Creat to meet you
in Scotland
all te best

Creat -

EDINBURGH
EDUCATION AND SOCIETY
SERIES

General Editor: Colin Bell

For Angie, who taught me more about the Highlands and Islands than any book.

Highland Games

The Making of the Myth

Grant Jarvie

EDINBURGH UNIVERSITY PRESS

© Grant Jarvie 1991

Edinburgh University Press
22 George Square, Edinburgh

Distributed in North America
by Columbia University Press
New York

Set in Linotron Palatino
by Koinonia Ltd, Bury, and
printed in Great Britain by
Page Bros   Ltd, Norwich

British Library Cataloguing
in Publication Data
Jarvie, Grant. 1955–
    The highland games: the making
    of the myth – (Edinburgh
    education and society series)
    1. Scottish highland games, history
    I. Title
    796.094111

ISBN 0 7486 0244 5

CONTENTS

List of Tables   vi

Preface   vii

Introduction: Sport, Dependency and the Scottish Highland
Gatherings   1
    Theory, Evidence and the Broader Context   2
    Dependency, Power and the Scottish Highland Gatherings   12

1 The Folk Origins of the Modern Highland Gatherings   15
    Processes of Unification and Anglicisation   16
    Wild Scots and Highlanders   22
    Highland Clans, Patriarchy and Feudalism   32

2 Cultural Transformation and Emigration   43
    Cultural Marginalisation   43
    Clearance and Emigration   47
    Cultural Transformation   56

3 The Sporting Landlords   62
    Balmorality and the Glamour of Backwardness   63
    The Popularisation Process   71

4 Problems of Modernity   81
    The Modern Highland Gatherings and Games   82
    Problems of Modernity   89
    Dominant and Residual Concerns   98

5 Urban Politics, Sporting Landlords and the Selection of
Tradition   101

Appendix I   106

Appendix II   107

Bibliography   108

Index   119

TABLES

1.1 Internal Clan Warfare during the Sixteenth Century   28
1.2 The MacCrummen Lineage, 1500–1980   37
1.3 Clan Military Power Prior to Culloden   41
2.1 Migration of Highland and Lowland Scots to British
     North America, 1760–1815   53
3.1 Highland Gatherings and Games, 1850–1910   72

PREFACE

Sport as an important aspect of Scottish culture has tended to be a neglected area of social research, though not of everyday social reality. One only needs to consider the place of sport in pub talk, everyday conversation, or even the emotional psyche of the nation around World Cup time to realise that a great deal of energy, banter and debate revolves around a question of sport. Whether it be Hampden Park, Dornoch Links, Braemar on Highland Games day or Murrayfield during Grand Slam Year, to be involved in sport in Scotland is to experience a sense of history and culture. Particularly striking are the larger-than-life characters such as Bill Shankly, Jock Stein, Bill Anderson, Donald Dinnie, Nancy Riach, Liz McCoglan, Lachie Stewart and many more – sporting men and women whose talents have found expression all over the world. Equally important are many thousands of us who, on a more recreational level, might enjoy the odd jog or bevy and fish supper after the game. In all its different forms, sport both constitutes and is constitutive of Scottish culture.

To take a critical view of sport or to attempt to situate sport within the broader context of history and social development is not to deny the voluntaristic and pleasurable dimensions of sport. The many hours and days that I spent observing and talking to Highland Games people in all corners of the Highlands served as a constant reminder that sporting observation and participation can be fun, pain and in general, mean different things to different people. However, the challenge lies in not denying such voluntaristic dimensions of sporting practice but in acknowledging that, for a broader understanding of why things are the way they are, it is necessary to relate sport to general features of social organisation and social development. Nor is it necessary to accept Ralph Miliband's view that sport itself is not conducive to any form of consciousness, for sport itself has always been an arena through which various groups have actively reworked their relationships and have responded to changing social conditions as a whole.

While a certain violence of abstraction pervades much of the sociology of sport material, *Highland Games: The Making of the Myth* attempts to provide an interweaving of theory and evidence. I certainly do not wish to support empiricism, nor indeed do I wish to argue for a withdrawal from epistemology. However, a retreat into epistemology must not be used as a means of sidestepping the necessity for historically grounded and theoretically guided observations. I am not arguing that it is irrelevant to find out how many men/women, rich/poor individuals engage in certain sports, but this sort of sporting data does not take us very far. Why, for example, do there tend to be Highland Gatherings in the Highlands and Highland Games overseas and in the Lowlands? The answer to such a question cannot come from mere reference to patterns of emigration or comments concerning the social composition of Highland Gatherings and Games. The question, in part, can only be answered by referring to the social structure of the Highland Gatherings and Games and how this has changed over time. Hence, an apparently simple question can take us straight into the heart of a complex debate about the social structure of the Highlands and its relationship to British political economy.

Seen in isolation the differences between various Highland Gatherings and Games may be considered as being insignificant. Yet viewed within the context of history and social development it is possible to shed light on present problems through a knowledge of the past. All cultures, sports and problems have histories involving people. You cannot begin to understand the Jim Baxter incident at Wembley in 1967 without any knowledge of Anglo-Scottish relations and struggles. A crucial point in all of this is that the same resources have not been universally available in these sporting struggles or quests for excitement. *Highland Games: The Making of the Myth* illustrates at least three notable measures of the power of different social groups to construct and negotiate sporting practices: (1) the capacity to structure Highland Gatherings in preferred ways and institutionalise these preferences in rules and organisations; (2) the capacity to establish selective traditions and rituals; and (3) the power to define a range of legitimate practices and meanings associated with Highland Gatherings such as amateurism and professionalism or Highland and Lowland. The resources which allow particular groups to do this are socially produced and are consequently negotiable.

In tracing the development of the Scottish Highland Gatherings, the text is organised as follows. The introduction is a necessary kind of prologue in which I briefly connect with some of the sociological and historical literature on sport before providing a synthesis of existing research on the Scottish Highland Gatherings. A number of theoretical points of departure are highlighted, and a number of classical problems or questions are raised. This initial synthesis paves the way for substantive material presented in Chapters 1, 2, 3 and 4. Chapter 1 considers the folk origins of the modern Highland Gatherings, while Chapter 2 considers the issues of cultural marginalisation and transformation within the context of the period 1740 to about 1850. Chapter 3 looks at the influence of the sporting landlords as a particularly powerful social class fraction which affected the development of not just the Highland Gatherings, but sport in the Highlands. Chapter 4 looks at the development of the modern Highland Gatherings and Games after about 1920. Implicit in all of this is the belief that an analysis of the Highland Gatherings is capable of providing insights into Scottish social structure, development and cultural identity. In conclusion, the major strands of the text are drawn together.

Various intellectual influences and sources of constructive advice have affected the outcome of this book. I am grateful to a number of people for their comments and encouragement. I would single out for special mention the work of Rick Gruneau and Eric Dunning whose influences on the text will be apparent. Their intellectual stimulus during the 1980s I found to be most rewarding. Special thanks must also go to David McCrone, Stephen Mennell, John Simpson and Tony Mason who indirectly provided me with help at various stages throughout this project. Gerry Redmond supplied me with Canadian and American material. The preparation of this text was funded through a grant provided by Warwick University. Carolyn Ison's thoroughness and patience was exemplary. This text would never have got off the ground or indeed have been completed without the help and assistance of all those people associated with the Highland Gatherings who either sent me material or were patient enough to talk to me. To all those people who provided me with information, whisky and endless stories, thank you. Needless to say, I am ultimately responsible for the final form this book has taken.

GRANT JARVIE
Brora, Sutherland

INTRODUCTION

SPORT, DEPENDENCY AND THE SCOTTISH HIGHLAND GATHERINGS

Over the last two decades or more, there has been a considerable interest in developing sociological and cultural explanations of sport. A number of Canadian, American and English social theorists have attempted to locate the development of various indigenous sporting forms within an analysis of their own culture (Gruneau, 1983; Dunning, Murphy and Williams, 1988; Harvey and Cantelon, 1988). One of the strengths of much of this work has been the attempt to situate the analysis of sport within the broader context of history and social development. In posing classical questions such as what the relationship is between sport and the prevailing social structure, and how sport has been affected by the historical epoch in which it moves, many writers have responded positively to the controversies concerning the inadequacy of those sociological accounts of sport that have been insensitive to historical concerns. Indeed, one of the hallmarks of much of the sociological work on sport that has emerged during the 1980s and early 1990s is that it has been rooted in historical concerns.

Yet much of the morass of literature that has been produced by British writers remains problematic in the sense that the theories and empirical materials pertaining to British sporting development and British culture remain firmly grounded in studies of England (Clarke and Critcher, 1985; Hargreaves,1986; Horne, Jary and Tomlinson, 1987). The old sleight of hand – British is English and English is British – is a problem acutely experienced by Irish, Welsh and Scottish social formations whose relative dependency continues to be mediated through Westminster. As such, it can be argued that the ethnocentralist nature of the sociology of sport and leisure literature in Britain is but a small reflection of a much broader problem of dependency and domination which exists within the 'divided' United Kingdom. While there have been some notable exceptions, what has generally been missing from both the sociological and cultural enquiries on sport in Britain is any sense of a peripheral presence in the form of Irish, Welsh or Scottish sporting traditions and experiences (Whitson, 1983; Cosgrove, 1985; Sugden, 1988, 1989; Holt, 1989; Jarvie, 1989). It is this peripheral presence which lies at the heart of the narrative on the Scottish Highland Gatherings presented in this book: narrative which attempts to locate the development of this sporting tradition within the broader context of Highland development in particular, and Scottish historiography in general.

The Scottish Highland Gatherings and Games as a particular cultural form consist of a number of complex traditions and customs which both mediate and are mediated by the unique pattern of social arrangements which have developed within Highland society and in Scottish culture generally. Kilted athletes, the voices of *émigrés* from all corners of the globe, the distinct sub-culture of the 'heavies', tartan-swathed dancers, the venison burger, the skirl of the pipes, sponsorship of the Tamnavulin Glenlivet Scottish Whisky circuit and the odd Clan Chief, invented or otherwise, are all part and parcel of a popular expression of modern Highland Gatherings and Games. This is itself nothing more than a contemporary expression of those groups of people who construct, control and negotiate the values, meanings and cultural practices associated with today's events: an expression which is clearly visible at Braemar, Lonach, Aboyne, Glenisla, Cowal and many other Highland Games.

If one is content merely to accept these events at face value, it is very easy to get caught up in the romantic Hollywood of the Highlands. Yet if one is interested enough to dig a little deeper and travel a little further, another interpretation of these Highland Gatherings and Games will present itself. The Highland Games at Glenelg provide an illustrative example of a loosely-formed more recreative Gathering in which tartanry, the skirl of the pipes and mass commercialisation are noticeable only by their absence. The social atmosphere and indeed social composition of this particular sporting form is more in keeping with the informal ceilidh than that of the commercial Highland Gatherings and Games circuit. Both of these interpretations are equally modern and yet one is continually marginalised and forgotten while the other is readily visible and kept alive in the consciousness of the tourist and the public at large.

THEORY, EVIDENCE AND THE BROADER CONTEXT

Richard Holt (1989: p. 357) has recently commented that sociologists have frequently complained about historical research which has lacked any theoretical grounding while historians have tended to feel that social theorists have not only tended to compress the diversity of the past into artificial, rigid categories, but have often dispensed with the empirical verification of their grand theories. In reality, just as sociology needs history, so too does theory need evidence. Purely theoretical accounts of sport are as unsatisfactory as those accounts of sporting practice which exude empirical findings without any theoretical grounding. The two are interdependent features of sociological analysis. As Elias (1978) points out, the constant interweaving between theory and evidence is the best defence against both the imposition of grand theory or scientific dogmas and empiricism without theoretical insight. It is precisely this atheoretical empiricism which has been characteristic of much of the work on the Scottish Highland Gatherings to date.

Published in 1927, the work of Iain Colquhoun and Hugh Machell, in *Highland Gatherings*, provides a vast amount of invaluable empirical data on three of the earliest and most prominent Highland Gatherings, namely the Braemar Royal Highland Gathering, the Luss Gathering and the Northern Meeting. The main empirical base for the research draws upon the minutes and records of selected Highland Society meetings up until about 1922. The research also makes use of various local newspapers such as the *Aberdeen Herald* and the *Inverness Courier*, the actual published programmes of the respective Gatherings, and the private papers and memoirs of the two authors. The available evidence is used to establish the origins of the respective Highland Gatherings and traces their development up until about 1926. In some instances, however, the authors, I believe, have attempted to hypothesise beyond the scope of the evidence provided.

The purpose of the Highland Gatherings, we are told, is for the laird and clansman, crofter and shepherd to meet on equal terms and keep alive the best sporting traditions of their 'races' (Colquhoun and Machell, 1927: p. 9). The past, whether it be real or invented, refers to a number of specific practices such as dancing traditional reels, tossing the caber, throwing the hammer and the traditional grand march by Highland pipers. Despite the hierarchy of occupations ranging from woodsman and farm labourer to skilled artisan and local landlord, the Highland Gatherings are regarded by these authors as a graphic symbol of a meritocracy in which it is taken for granted that all compete under equal conditions with the available rewards accruing to the most highly skilled.

There are three chapters in the book devoted to the origin and history of the three particular Highland Gatherings up until 1926. First, there is the Braemar Royal Highland Society Gathering, dating back to the eleventh century, which claims to be descended from a Gathering organised by Malcolm Ceann-Mor. Secondly, the Luss Gathering is described which, we are told, was first held in 1875 and owes its inception to the voluntary action of the landed gentry and many local farmers, all of whom belonged to the Luss Company of Dumbartonshire volunteers. Finally, there is a well documented account of the Northern Meeting which was inaugurated on 11 June 1788. Let me begin by briefly describing the narrative presented with regard to these Highland Gatherings.

In Italy and Greece, from ancient times up until the present day, historians have managed to uncover and preserve many authentic records and stories of Roman and Greek culture. Yet in the case of Scottish sporting culture, the authentic information in the form of records of meetings, newspaper accounts and various local histories only spans about two hundred years. Certainly with regard to the Northern Meeting, the *minutes* of the meeting clearly indicate that its point of origin dates precisely from 11 June 1788 (N/M, Minutes: 11 June 1788). The richness of this source of information is unquestionable. Consider some of the following resolutions that were passed at this inaugural convention:

1. That the meeting shall be named the NORTHERN MEETING.

2. That every Gentleman or Lady, being the Head of the Family, who is or shall become a Constituent Member of this Meeting, shall pay to one Secretary, the sum of ONE GUINEA Yearly, for the public Purposes of the Meeting; and that all such Members as shall absent themselves shall pay double the sum (excepting officers below the Rank of Field-Officers, who may be necessarily absent on duty).

3. That this meeting do name the Stewards and Secretary for the Year, and do accordingly nominate and appoint. A Penrose Cumming of Altyre; James Fraser of Culduthel; Edward Fraser of Relickm and Donald Macleod of Greanies, Esgs, to be Stewards for the first Meeting, and Doctor John Alves Physician here to be secretary.

4. That the whole Business of the Meeting shall be conducted by the Stewards and Secretary, conformable to the General Regulations now laid down. That they shall alternately act as Toast-master and Croupier at the Entertainments, and as master of ceremonies at the Ball Room; and that the whole Gentlemen and Ladies of the Meeting, shall support the Authority of the Stewards.

5. That the whole Company, Ladies and Gentlemen, do Dine together, and that it is to be understood as a Regulation, that they do all come to the table dressed for the Ball in the Evening.

6. That the Dinner be on the Table each Day precisely at Four o'clock. That the Ladies having retired, the Bill shall be called for by the Two Stewards, who do not act as Toast-master and Croupier for the day, at Half past six o'clock, and be proportioned by them, and collected by the Secretary, as soon as it can be proportioned.

7. That immediately after the Bill is settled and paid, the Gentlemen do adjourn to the Ball Room.

8. That the dancing do commence each Night precisely by Eight o'clock and stop precisely by Twelve.

9. That the next meeting shall commence on Monday, the Twenty-Seventh of October, and continue to have an Entertainment and a Ball on that day, the Tuesday, Wednesday, Thursday and Friday following; and that on the forenoon of Saturday, the Gentlemen of the Meeting, shall assemble at Beverly's, receive the Secretaries

Accounts, chuse new Stewards and Secretary, appoint the following Years Meeting, determine any Petition for Admission of New Members, and do any other Business that may respect the meeting.

It was precisely this type of documentation that was commented upon by Elias (1983: p. 5) when considering the work of the historian L. Von Ranke. In agreement with Ranke, Elias insisted upon the compilation of original evidence. The documents, the original sources of information are in many cases the very substance of history. Without this meticulous documentation of reliable historical sources, there is a very real danger of subjective interpretation and misrepresentation of subject matter. The historian runs the danger of selecting from the events of the past in the light of what he or she approves or disapproves in the present. Not that meticulous documentation on its own is sufficient. It needs to be guided, informed and orientated towards a body of reliable theory.

The same kind of careful documentation characterises much of Colquhoun and Machell's discussion on the history of the Braemar Royal Highland Society Gathering from the early nineteenth century until the early twentieth century. It is interesting that the Braemar Royal Highland Society takes as its point of origin a meeting of the Braemar Wrights Society in January 1816 (Colquhoun and Machell, 1927). The early membership of this society consisted primarily of skilled manual workers, mostly carpenters, who developed it as a form of collective social insurance in the absence of any welfare state. This early form of trade union or friendly society carried kinship and friendship a practical step further by organising social relief in times of hardship for the sick, the elderly, widows and orphans amongst its membership.

By 1826 the Society had been transformed into the Braemar Highland Society. By that time, too, the social composition of this particular set of social practices had also changed. The quarterly meetings were now presided over by the local laird. By 1826, although the distribution of 'kind' remained one of the primary functions of the Society, its other tasks had come to include the preservation of the kilt, together with the language and cultural interests of the Highlands (Colquhoun and Machell, 1927: p. 85). A paradoxical situation had, in other words, emerged where many of those who were initially responsible for the destruction of the distinct Highland way of life after the 1745 rebellion were the very people who became primarily responsible for the preservation of many of the cultural artefacts and customs of a previous social order.

By 1831, the Vice Presidents of the Society included Lord Elcho, Sir David Kinlock, Sir Thomas Lauder and Sir William Cumming, all titled landowners belonging to a particular social class and bonded together by a number of marks of similarity including social rank and ownership of property, amongst others. By 1832, the first athletic contests took place on the last Thursday of August with £5 prize money going to each winner of the five major contests which included putting the stone, throwing the hammer, tossing the caber, running, and length of military service (Colquhoun and Machell, 1927: p. 86). That same year another landowner, the Marquis of Caermarthen, presented each of his gamekeepers with a complete Highland costume of his own Dunblane tartan (Viscount Dundee being one of his subsidiary titles) (Colquhoun and Machell, 1927: p. 85). Other Society members followed suit, with the Earl of Fife and Farquharson of Invercauld presenting each of their estate members with a costume of their respective clan tartans, namely Duff and Farquharson (Colquhoun and Machell, 1927: p. 85). The trend was repeated in later years by Queen Victoria who presented Royal Stuart tartans to many of her retainers at Balmoral.

Between 1847 and 1900, the popularity of the Highland Gatherings was in no small way due to the patronage bestowed on the Braemar Highland Society by Queen Victoria. By 1866 the Society had become known as the Braemar Royal Highland Society. As the reigning monarch, Queen Victoria invited the Society to hold a number of gatherings on her estate at Balmoral; during her reign, Highland Gatherings were held at Balmoral, amongst other years, in 1859, 1887, 1890, 1898 and 1899 (Colquhoun and Machell, 1927: p. 64). Indeed, Colquhoun and Machell (1927: p. 65) note that, in 1899, the Queen provided luncheon and dinner for all the Fife, Invercauld, Lonach and the Queen's Own Balmoral Highlanders. The authors also note that due to the fact that the running race to the top of Craig Choinnich was seen to 'seriously affect the constitution of the competitors', the Queen herself intervened in 1842 to stop the run, lest there be loss of life (Colquhoun and Machell, 1927: p. 70).

Despite this careful documentation of evidence from the early nineteenth century onwards, in an attempt to enhance the origin of this Highland tradition the authors argue that the origin of the Highland Gatherings in general, and of the Braemar Gathering in particular, can be traced back to at least the eleventh century. Legend, they say, has it that King Malcolm Ceann-Mor (1058-93) called the clans to the Braes of Mar to select by competition the fastest athletes amongst the clansfolk in order that they might act as postal runners to carry messages for the King throughout the Highlands and Lowlands of Scotland. With this in mind, it is argued that the King organised a hill race to the summit of Craig Choinnich overlooking Braemar. A somewhat lengthy account of this race is provided by Colquhoun and Machell (1927: p. 60):

> The race became more and more exciting. Some of the hindermost had even given up; but all those who were not despairingly far behind put forth thew and sinew, and pressed close after each other ready to take advantage of every accident. The two M'Gregors had indeed left the others considerably behind ... young M'Gregor sprang forward with unabated energy, passing the other one after another ... Now they came in sight of their goal – now the judges encouraged them by their cheers – now they seem renewed again in

vigour. The youngest put his whole sould forth; the oldest summoned up all the strength of his tougher frame. Terribly pressed he was yet determined to gain and stretched out his arm to impede the motion of his rival, but felt nothing. They had only four yards to go. He looked to the side expecting to see him on the ground. At that moment the tartans grazed the skin on his knee. His brother had leaped forward below his outstretched arm. Furious he bounded on and fell, his hand clutching with iron grasp the kilt of his rival. He was two yards from the flag and his strength exhausted. He could not drag the other's prostrate body one step, and now he saw the hindermost fast approaching. Quick as thought, loosening the belt of his kilt he resigned it to the other. He reached the signal with three feeble springs, seized the staff and threw it in the air. The youngest had reached the top in three minutes. Thus the origin of the Braemar Games attached itself to the days of Malcolm of the big head.

One of the major problems that any researcher faces when trying to pinpoint the exact origin of events such as the Highland Gatherings is the fragmentary nature of the evidence. Highland tradition itself helps to explain this problem since so many of the legends, customs, and traditions of the Highland communities tended to be passed on from generation to generation by word of mouth rather than being written down. The historian Isobel Grant (1939: p. 479) develops this point when she comments upon one of the key problems which have pervaded many of the early accounts of Highland history. On a number of occasions, remarks Grant, the narratives of the Scots chroniclers from the eleventh century onwards have been misguided by the desire to enhance the origins of the country's Highland institutions and customs in comparison with those of England by tracing them back to an earlier period.

This is not to say that the event on Craig Choinnich either did or did not take place, but merely that there is not enough empirical evidence to argue categorically that this was the point of origin of the first gathering. It certainly could not have been a *Highland* Gathering of the clans, since the word Highlander did not emerge until the fourteenth-century (Brown, 1843: pp. 11-12). Nor can it be said that this particular event served the same function as the eighteenth-century Highland Society Gatherings in terms of the distribution of kind or the provision of a social event on the calendar of the landed gentry and local aristocracy. It would be far more accurate to argue that there is a possibility that the modern Highland Gatherings might be descended from a number of particular antecedent cultural and sporting events, some of which may date back to at least the eleventh century. The folk origins of the modern Highland Gatherings are explored further in Chapter 1.

Anyone who reads Colquhoun and Machell's account of the various Highland Gatherings is left in no doubt about the influence of a particular social class in shaping the late-eighteenth and early-nineteenth-century gatherings. A certain relationship between the local landed gentry and various Highland Society Gatherings has already been mentioned. A further flavour of the proceedings can be acquired from the following extracts from Colquhoun and Machell (1927: pp. 26-9):

> It must be remembered that athletes and sportsmen are two different characters. They are frequently combined in one person; indeed it is difficult to find a true athlete who is not a sportsman in the accepted terms of those who have acquired the cachet of a public school or the imprimatur of a leading university.
>
> Let us return from all of this to the quiet seclusion of some Scottish glen, where a few days before the great meetings a handful of hardworking farm hands are practising the caber or shot. Do you think the bookmakers are dreamt of in their philosophy? Could anything be more incongruous with its surroundings than a deafening din of 3 to 1 Starkey or evens Maitland while these honest Highlanders were tossing the caber before royalty in the arena at Braemar?
>
> Twenty thousand crowd at Braemar now annually raises its unanimous voice to welcome our good King George V ... Let us hope that never, even in another two hundred years, will it be necessary for the loyal subjects of our sovereign to raise the standard.

The initial discussion of the Highland Gatherings has raised certain questions about the importance of the empirical base upon which theoretical assumptions rest. The strength of Colquhoun and Machell's work lies in their empirical grounding of the subject matter from the eighteenth century onwards. I have argued, though, that owing to the lack of concrete evidence regarding the past Highland oral traditions it is impossible to establish the validity of the claim that the Highland Gatherings existed as early as or before the eleventh century. I shall develop this position further through considering the work of David Webster.

David Webster's interest in the Scottish Highland Games seems to have grown out of a degree of personal involvement with the Highland Games circuit. This intimate knowledge of the Highland Games led to the publication of *Scottish Highland Games* in 1959 – subsequently revised, extended and published as a second edition in 1973. In the introduction, the reader is led to believe that the promise of the book lies in the research compiled from authentic records which have enabled the author to describe the development of the Highland Gatherings and their effect on the social and cultural patterns of Scotland.

Yet despite a certain sensitivity to historical concerns within the text, like Colquhoun and Machell the author tends to push the historical narrative beyond a point at which there is original documentary evidence to substantiate his various claims. For instance, on the question of origin, Webster makes reference to an event at Bailemuirn which allegedly took place during the eighth-century Pictish period of control in ancient

Caledonia. More particularly Webster (1973: p. 9) argues that:

A very definite resemblance to present-day ceremonies can be seen, but instead of having a chieftain and guest of honour as we sometimes have today, they had druids to bless the games and be honoured guests while the King or chieftain actually took charge of the proceedings, signalling the start of the races and so on ... A march past of the procession has always been an integral part of the gatherings and even on these early occasions they were greatly appreciated. The druids arrived in processions and on reaching the gates of Rth, or enclosure, the officer or guard would beat on the boss of his shield and a salute would be blown. After the King had received his guests and the crowd has assembled, huge jars of drink would be set out for the spectators.

While it would enhance the heritage of the Highland Gatherings to be able to trace them back to this historical epoch, a number of points prevent us from being absolutely certain about this question of origin. The first point is that no other research on the Highland Gatherings has been able to verify that the Bailemuirn event ever took place. A second reason for rejecting Bailemuirn rests with the druidical cultural practice of versification. The Picts strictly adhered to the druidical religious order, which strictly forbade the use of writing as a means of passing on folklore and customs from generation to generation. Instead, the druids practised the cultivation of memory as a means of retaining knowledge and maintaining a secrecy about their way of life (Skene, 1937). The traditions and customs were passed on by oral means which, in part, might help to explain many of the silences alluded to earlier.

In the first chapter, entitled 'The Development of the Scottish Highland Games', Webster traces the development of the Games from what he takes to be their point of origin through to the first half of the twentieth century (Webster, 1973: pp. 9-13). This entire historical epoch spanning over eleven hundred years is covered in five pages of narrative. Despite this superficial explanation, the author does, in places, attempt to make tentative links with various dominant moments in Scottish history. For instance, commenting upon the defeat of the Jacobite Army at the battle of Culloden in 1746, Webster (1973: p.10) notes:

Bonnie Prince Charlie and his Highland hosts watched their men compete in athletics while passing time between skirmishes, but the battle of Culloden in 1746, brought a drastic end to the aspirations of the prince and the '45 rebellion. Repression followed, and in the Act of Proscription, a ban was placed on the carrying of arms, the wearing of the kilt, the playing of the bagpipes and the gathering together of persons. Offenders were either deported or embarked for the colonies voluntarily. By one Act of Parliament, many of the cultural traditions of the country were severed.

By the end of the eighteenth century, Webster (1973: p. 11) goes on, it became clear that a determined attempt was needed if traditional aspects of Highland culture were to be retained. To this end various Highland Societies began to play their part. The first Society Gathering took place, not in the Highlands but at Falkirk in 1781. In 1819, the St Fillans Society promoted a full-scale games with piping, dancing and athletics. The first Crieff Games took place on 18 August 1870, the same year as the first Comrie Games were established. Records of these early Society Games, notes Webster (1973: p 11), make it clear that the prime function was to arrange social gatherings for the local nobility or gentry. In this sense, these Highland Society Gatherings were no different from the 1788 Northern Meeting mentioned earlier.

It is one of the strengths of *Scottish Highland Games* (1973) that in this first chapter Webster does not lose sight of some dominant moments in history which have, in part, helped to shape or transform this Highland tradition. It is important, though, not to lose sight of the fact that such dominant moments in history were in fact brought about by groups or figurations of people. A failure both to personify and to conceptualise the very complex way in which both the Scottish social formation and the Highland Gatherings have developed has led Webster to a very simplistic, empirical, atheoretical, descriptive type of analysis.

This is not to say that there is no place in sociological research for empirical studies. In all cases these are indispensable, but the point of issue, according to Elias (1956), rests with the theoretical hypothesis upon which such empirical studies are undertaken. Empirical research without theory often facilitates only limited access to the problems of 'deep' structures, social change and many other sociological problems. The theoretical framework of sociology needs to go beyond simple description in an attempt fully to comprehend the social significance of the phenomena being studied.

A greater sensitivity in Webster's work to such notions as power, culture and dependency would have provided a fuller explanation of the significance of the Highland Games within the development of Scotland as a social formation. For instance, it could be argued that the significance of Culloden was not that it was a catastrophic defeat for the Jacobite army, but that what distinguishes Culloden from previous Jacobite defeats was that it preceded a massive assault on the social and political institutions of clanship. The abolition of the chiefs' judicial powers over their clans was a major factor in the destruction of an old way of life (Hunter, 1976). These developments were accompanied by a determined attempt to modernise the Highland economy and integrate the region and its people into a social order from which they had hitherto kept aloof. The demise of an old social order gave rise to a new social formation in which landlords were losing the characteristics of chieftains or lairds on easygoing terms with tenants and were driven, in part, by economic circumstances which placed a much greater emphasis on economic bonds than on the traditional bonding of kinship.

Whether we are concerned with the social history of the ancient Picts, kinship networks such as clans, or individual chiefs and landlords, the fact remains that we are dealing with groups of people who are connected together in a very complex web of interdependence. For a long period in the social formation of Highland society, people were connected over and over again by the interdependence of chief – chieftain – tacksman – clansfolk. At yet another level the Grants, Mackenzies, Mackays and Macdonalds and many other clans formed particular webs of interdependence both among themselves and with each other which contributed not only to the social and political institutions of clanship but also to a particular local form of more general bonding to the royal house of Stuart. Such social formations are just as real as the individual people forming them. Yet, as Elias (1983: p. 14) indicates, what many people find difficult to grasp is the fact that these groups of people can have a slower rate of transformation than the individuals who comprise them.

The old social order of the clan was not a phenomenon that existed outside of the individuals forming it. Individuals, whether it be chief or chieftain, tacksman or tenant, crofter or cotter did not exist independently or outside of the social structure which they formed together. To take an example from Webster (1973: p.15), the author comments upon the emotional bonding between the present royal monarch and the Braemar Highland Gathering. Yet it is important not to separate the individual royal position of Queen Elizabeth from the longer process by which the royal position or monarch came to be associated with the Highland Gatherings. In the same way, Webster (1973: p. 25) notes the level of excellence attained by one *émigré*, George Goldie, in whose honour the Princeton Caledonia Games of 1873 were inaugurated. Again, it is important not to distinguish between the achievements of one *émigré* George Goldie, and the longer process by which *émigrés* came to be associated with various Caledonian Games abroad. Finally, one should not distinguish between the association of one landlord such as Lord Elcho with the Braemar Royal Highland Gathering and the longer process by which landlords in general came to be associated specifically with Highland Gatherings and generally with the Highland social formation. Each of these illustrations helps to explain the same point, namely that, while it might be possible to distinguish between individuals and their social position such as royalty, landlord, emigrant or chief, in reality the two positions are not separate. Individual landlords may have a relative autonomy but only in so far as the limits associated with their social position allow them. In particular, the degree of socially-generated autonomy of his/her social position sets limits upon the individual power of even the strongest clan chief or landlord. That, of course, is because a social position is a position of one individual or group of individuals in relation to other individuals or groups. In other words, although sociological tradition makes it seem that social positions exist entirely independently of individual human beings, that is not in reality the case even where the relative autonomy of social positions is maximised through crystallisation as formalised written roles. This is because such prescriptions only achieve human reality through being enacted by independent human beings.

The subject matter of this initial discussion on the Highland Gatherings strikes directly at what might be called the conventional wisdom on the subject. To date, research in this area has been dominated by the work of David Webster and the writings of Iain Colquhoun and Hugh Machell. The term 'conventional wisdom' is not meant here in any derogatory sense. On the contrary, the works of these writers provides an invaluable source of empirical information. Yet the empiricist, atheoretical framework of analysis used in both instances is unsatisfactory if we are to go beyond merely descriptive expositions of this Highland tradition.

DEPENDENCY, POWER AND THE SCOTTISH HIGHLAND GATHERINGS

The challenge of the Scottish Highland Gatherings lies precisely in acknowledging not only the voluntaristic, pleasurable dimensions of this sporting tradition but also in perceiving that this cultural form has emerged from the unique struggles and development peculiar to Scottish society. Sporting culture, like all forms of culture, is itself created not within some sort of social vacuum but within the broader context of history and social development. As such, sporting images, sporting relations of power, sporting cultural identity and the ability to define the very nature of sporting practices in Scotland is something that not only works for or against particular sporting actors and players, but also operates through the differential capacity of different class fractions, genders and nations to define the rules which govern cultural production and the selection of tradition. In situating the development of the Scottish Highland Gatherings within this broader context, the narrative as it is presented in this book revolves around four interrelated phases of development. They are:

1. A stage which lasted from at least the eleventh century until about 1750. During this stage of development many of the cultural artefacts upon which today's Highland Gatherings are dependent existed in various antecedent forms. They contributed to a somewhat violent, materially impoverished way of life which, in part, revolved around a fusion of patriarchal-feudal forces which gave rise to the Highland clan formation.

2. A stage which lasted from about 1740 until about 1850. At least three important processes affected the development of the Highland Gatherings during this stage (a) a process of cultural marginalisation which resulted in the relative destruction of the original Highland way of life and the cultural artefacts which contributed to it; (b) a process of emigration which resulted in many Highland customs being transported with the émigré to North America in particular and (c) an initial stage of cultural transformation during which many

Highland and Friendly Societies actually encouraged the further development of a number of Highland Gatherings.

3. A stage which lasted from about 1840 until about 1920 which resulted in the Highland Gatherings becoming inextricably linked with images of 'Balmorality', loyalty and royalty. This contributed to, not just the popularisation of the Highland Gatherings, but also the popularisation of the Highlands in general as a leisure playground for the 'sporting landlords'.

4. A stage which lasted from about 1910 until the present day during which the Highland Gatherings and Games experienced problems of modernity. A number of multi-faceted developments such as incipient bureaucratisation, rationalisation, increasing professionalisation and changing class relations all contributed to a dominant interpretation of the Highland Gatherings. And yet the residual images of tartanry, clans and landlords continued to be produced and reproduced within the changing nexus of Highland and Scottish development.

Implicit within this analysis of the Highland Gatherings is the belief that such a study can provide insights into a number of secondary problem areas. I do not intend at this point to provide an in-depth discussion on these concerns but merely to highlight a number of significant points of departure. Firstly, there is the issue of dependency and uneven development. The idea that social structures and patterns of social development are greatly influenced by relations of power and dependency that occur between a metropole and a hinterland is certainly one that, at different levels, lends itself to an explanation of Highland and Scottish development. One of the constant themes within Highland political economy has been that of community instability and the effect which a tenurial system of land control has had on past and present social structures. That the question of the sporting landlords is still regarded as a key question in the political economy of the Highlands and engenders considerable emotion is no more than a reflection of what many commentators regard as a major but unanswered question: who ought to own and control the land of the Scottish periphery? In a European context, Highland Scotland is perhaps unique in that the bulk of the Highlands is owned and controlled by a handful of beneficiaries who, irrespective of their involvement with land as a productive resource, have an influence on local communities which many regard as being disproportionate, in terms of the standards that pertain in other European countries.

Secondly, in agreement with Foster-Carter (1985: p. 113), I would suggest that dependency theory has been overtly economistic, plagued by various dualisms, and has failed to pay due attention to unique and varying problems of cultural dependency such as those involved in the selection of tradition and cultural identity. Historians have maintained that some societies preserve what they regard as significant events in a manifest form, so that it is relatively easy to reconstruct the broad outlines of the past. Other societies bury their past in forms which are often difficult to unravel. Yet cultural change and the selection of tradition is often a polite euphemism for process by which some traditions and customs are driven out of the centre of popular life. Rather than simply falling into disuse, some traditions are actively pushed aside so that others can take their place. A number of writers have been careful to point out that while nations may become culturally dependent upon symbols and invented traditions, such symbols and traditions are, in fact, constructed and formally instituted by people who themselves seek to inculcate certain values and norms (Hall, 1981; Hobsbawn, 1984; Nairn, 1981, 1988). Yet the centrepiece of any discussion on dependency must be the uneven balance of power between the various groups who enter into such a relationship. The notion of power has proved to be a fruitful analytical concept for many social and political theorists. In his earlier work, Poulantzas in particular tended to view power entirely in class terms. In *State, Power and Socialism* (1978) he concedes that relations of power do not exhaust class relations and must go a certain way beyond them. One of the major advantages of the approach to power adopted here is the open-ended framework which allows for not only social class explanations of power, but also a multitude of other dynamic power relations. Power in this sense is a structural characteristic of all relationships. As long as people are dependent upon one another, whether it be as a function of emotional, political or economic bonds, there will always be a balance of power within and between different social groups of clans or nation-states or cores and hinterlands. This relational practice of power and dependency operates at a number of different levels. The crucial point is that dependency is a relational phenomenon which in practice operates at variably interpenetrating levels.

Guided by such concerns, the following questions are central to the analysis of the Scottish Highland Gatherings presented in this text: What is the relationship between the Highland Gatherings and the prevailing social structure? How have the Highland Gatherings been affected by Highland and Scottish development? Why did this tradition suddenly become popular after about 1840? What is the relationship between the Highland Gatherings and various cultures such as the clans, landlords and *émigrés*? In what way do the Highland Gatherings reproduce a certain Scottish cultural identity? Is this Highland tradition an invented tradition, or is it that the selection of traditions reflected in this sporting form have been influenced by a dominant and yet somewhat changing figuration of people who have had the power to influence and control the agenda at these Scottish Highland Gatherings? In addressing these issues, this account of the Scottish Highland Gatherings encompasses some of the most basic questions that might be asked concerning Scottish cultural identity, dependency and social structure.

1

THE FOLK ORIGINS OF THE MODERN HIGHLAND GATHERINGS

There was perhaps never any change of national manners so quick, so great and so general as that which operated in the Highlands by the late conquest and subsequent laws ... The clans retain little now of their original character. Their ferocity of temper is softened, their military ardour is extinguished, their dignity of independence is depressed, their contempt of government subdued, and their reverence for their chiefs abated (Johnson, 1924: p. 51).

It is within the broader context of the social relations which characterised the Highland clan formation that many of the folk origins of the modern Highland Gatherings may be found and understood. A particular way of life existed in the Highlands until about 1746, after which the British state's post-Culloden policies gradually marginalised and eventually transformed the traditions, social structure and experiences of those people who lived out their lives within the Highland social formation. Yet it is not the post-Culloden phase of development which is the central concern of this chapter, but the period up until about 1750. The evidence provided above by Dr Samuel Johnson certainly alludes to a Highland way of life in which the Highland clans were ferocious, independent, contemptuous of government and in reverence of their chiefs. The basis for such an interpretation stems, in part, from the dominant perception of the Highland way of life as being primitive, violent and an increasing embarrassment to the more civilised people within the British social formation. Such perceptions, at least in part, invariably rest upon the power to define history. To control a people, first control their history. Histories of many social formations have often been written at the expense of the marginalisation of subordinate social fractions. As a 'destroyer of myths', it is part of the role of the sociologist to question such interpretations.

More specifically, this chapter attempts to establish the fact that many of the traditions which are so central to today's Highland Gatherings did in fact exist within a Highland social formation which existed before about 1750. The wearing of tartan dress, the playing of the pio-baireached, hill-running, and Highland dancing are all examples of cultural practices which existed before the middle of the eighteenth century and form the core of existing Highland Gatherings such as Lonach, Braemar and Glenisla. Without the inclusion of such practices, albeit in their modern forms, today's Highland Gatherings would be recognised as something other than Highland. When asked what are the requirements of a traditional Highland Gathering, the secretary of the Glenisla Highland Gathering replied (Glenisla: 18 August 1986): 'Piping, highland dancing, hillrunning and heavy events. These are the main things, and another thing which I don't think is adhered to enough today is people who are organising and running the games should all wear Highland dress.'

I think it is important to emphasise that the following analysis is not meant to be a detailed social history of the Highland social formation. My primary intention in this chapter is to establish the fact that an initial phase in the development of the Highland Gatherings took place between approximately the eleventh century and about 1750. A secondary concern is to illustrate that many antecedent forms and practices, which have subsequently developed into what are today the modern Highland Gatherings, did in fact contribute to the social and political institutions of a Highland way of life which differentiated itself from a more powerful Lowland formation. At the centre of this Highland social formation was the Highland clan, a particular figuration, characterised in part by a patriarchal – feudal set of social relations.

PROCESSES OF UNIFICATION AND ANGLICISATION

While the narrative in this instance begins during the eleventh century, it would be misleading and indeed incorrect to suggest that various processes and figurations had not already influenced the relatively fluid structure of the Scottish social formation before this period in history. With reference to the origins of the modern Highland Gatherings, it is not necessary to provide an in-depth analysis of the Scottish people much before the reign of Malcolm Ceann-Mor (1058-1093). By this stage, the existing social formation had already undergone a complex developmental process leading to the emergence of a number of relatively independent social fractions each having a greater or lesser degree of power.

It is possible to identify five broad, relatively independent social fractions which occupied the territory now called Scotland before the eleventh century. The Picts, writes Gregory (1836: p. 2), being the original Caledonians, continued to be the most powerful group north of the 'Firths' up until the sixth century. At the beginning of this period, the Irish Scots, or Dalriads, developed settlements in both Kintyre and Argyll. The Strathclyde Britons occupied the land of Cumbria stretching all the way from Dumbarton over to Carlisle, plus a vast area south of the Solway Firth which today is referred to as Cumbria and Westmorland. However, conquests by more powerful Anglo-Saxon groups meant that much of the territory controlled by the Britons, together with Northumberland and

Lothian, subsequently came under the control of the Anglo-Saxon group which had come up from the south. The final group to influence the development of the Scottish social formation during this early period were the Norsemen who continually attacked the inhabitants of the Western Isles from at least the eighth century. Some of the oldest Highland clans take their point of origin from Somerled, a vassal of the King of Norway who emerged as a distinct threat to the Scottish monarchy during the twelfth century.

An initial unification process took place between about AD 843 and about AD 1050. This development had mainly been the work of the Irish Scots or Dalriads who had in part united the relatively independent groups under Kenneth MacAlpine, the first King of the Scots (843-?). This initial unification process became a necessary development for the Picts, Irish Scots, Anglo-Saxons, and Strathclyde Britons who were continually being attacked by the more powerful Norse raiders. However, it would be wrong to think of this initial Scottish formation as a unified state. Despite their relative allegiance to the monarchy, there was, as yet, no notion of law that could be applied to all the different groups. Each of them had distinct characteristics and interests. Each of them had a degree of power relative to the others and each was prone to rebellion.This nominal unification was subject to a succession of tensions and strains as a result of the degree of power which any one of the relatively independent groups exercised within the union at any particular period. During phases in which the Norse threat of domination was high, the bonding of these Scottish groups was strong. During periods in which the threat of domination was reduced, unification amongst the Picts, Irish Scots, Anglo-Saxons, and Strathclyde Britons was prone to degrees of instability. It might be argued that the most striking features of this nominal unification were the low level of cohesion which existed and the strength of the centrifugal forces which tended to contribute to disintegration.

Furthermore, it would be far too simplistic to argue that, at this stage, the social differentiation amongst these past social factions revolved around a distinct set of Highland and Lowland or Celtic and non-Celtic social relations. Certain factors which gave rise to such a social differentiation began to appear as a result of a second process, an anglicisation process, which further emerged during the rule of the Canmore Kings. The succession of Canmore Kings up until the end of the thirteenth century marked a very definite and important epoch in the social and economic development of Scotland. A number of interrelated factors marked the evolution of the Lowlanders as a particularly powerful force whose values and way of life became gradually more closely connected with the affluent south as opposed to the more mountainous wild regions of the north.

By the eleventh century, the Gaelic language was spoken throughout most of Scotland. The power of the Dalriadic tribe had procured a Gaelic hegemony under what proved to be the last of the Gaelic-speaking monarchs, Malcolm Ceann-Mor. A paradoxical situation emerged when the monarch went to the English royal house for a Queen who held the values and beliefs of a more Anglo-Norman civilisation as opposed to the traditions of Gaelic Scotland. There can be no doubt that the marriage of Malcolm Ceann-Mor to Queen Margaret in 1058 marked a decisive phase in a process of change by which the Anglo-Norman figuration became the more dominant influence upon the Scottish throne. According to the *Old Statistical Account of Scotland* (1831 Vol 12, p. 127), the marriage in 1058 marked the beginning of an anglicisation process which eventually led to the marginalisation of Gaelic culture and an increasing cultural dependency upon a more dominant metropolitan culture. This anglicisation process continues today. For instance, in the case of Argyll, though it is still Highland in both a topographical and figurational sense, the permeating effects of this anglicisation process have meant that the people, once members of an independent Gaelic-speaking culture, are now linked with the English-speaking West of Scotland linguistically, commercially and, in some cases, sentimentally. The last battle to be fought on British soil, the Battle of Culloden (1746), marked the end of an intense period of struggle against the marginalisation of the Highland way of life.

If the emergence of an anglicisation process was one factor which eventually led to a Highland/Lowland social differentiation, a second factor was the decision taken by Malcolm Ceann-Mor, and the subsequent Canmore Kings, to remove the royal court from its Highland seat in Perth to a more southerly, Lowland seat in Dunfermline. One of the unintended consequences of this action was an increase in the level of violence experienced in the north of Scotland. In those areas of the north such as the glens and the valleys, far removed from royal jurisdiction, it became increasingly difficult to practise the same levels of law and order that prevailed in the south. As Browne (1841: Vol. 2, p. 127) indicates, the transfer of the seat of government to the south meant that the administration and practice of law became either inoperative or feebly enforced in the north. The people of the north gave themselves up to violence and turbulence and revenged in person any insults or injuries which the law did not attend to. In short, the removal of the Scottish court from the north to the south facilitated, in part, a process which led to the inhabitants of the north developing another formation in order to protect themselves from attacks, and also to attack aggressive or weak neighbours. This process contributed to the emergence between the fourteenth and eighteenth centuries of the Highland clan formation, a relatively unique figuration which developed a specific set of social relations and practices.

Perhaps the greatest catalyst in this period of change was the development of further forms of feudal control. This, probably more than any other factor, created the emergent social differentiation which, in the fourteenth century, expressed itself in Highland and Lowland figurational terms. Feudalism was specifically viewed as a mechanism by which the monarchy could consolidate its power through a set of feudal relations. The whole feudal edifice functioned to support the monarch at its apex as the ultimate ruler of all land and the sole fountainhead of all justice. Particularly in the more southerly Lowlands, this contributed to a further unification spurt whereby the fusion of Anglo-Saxons, Strathclyde Britons and fragments of several other social fractions gave rise to a relatively unified Lowland group of people. Yet in the north, the feudal relationship between landlord and tenant was mediated by a partriarchal relationship which existed between the Celtic tribal chiefs and the clansfolk. The policies of the succession of Canmore Kings were violently resisted by the people of the north. In many ways the entire history of what was to become the Highland social formation during the period between the eleventh and the eighteenth centuries revolved around the tension between the centrifugal tendencies of the Highland chiefs and the destabilisation forces which resulted, in part, from the process of anglicisation.

Aspects of Elias's (1982: pp. 13-90) discussion on the dynamics of feudalisation are directly applicable to a deeper understanding of the mechanisms involved in this process of destabilisation. The state of military, economic and transport arrangements during this stage of Scottish development left the ruling monarchs, in this case the Canmore Kings, with little choice but to delegate power to a network of Highland chiefs. Neither of these groups were restricted by an oath of allegiance or loyalty to the central authority. Consequently, whoever was delegated power within any particular territory was in effect ruler of that area (Elias, 1982: p.17). As soon as the central power showed signs of weakness, the Highland chiefs as territorial landlords sought to demonstrate their independence from the central authority and their own ability to rule within their own clan territories. That is to say that one of the essential characteristics of feudalism involved a process whereby centrifugal pressures became dominant over centripetal pressures, with the result that effective power became concentrated in the hands of the local Highland chiefs.

Clearly, no single factor led to the differentiation between what were to develop into relatively autonomous Highland and Lowland cultures within the Scottish social formation. A number of other factors in addition to those discussed so far might also be mentioned. Some writers have explained the processes which subsequently led to the social differentiation between the people of the north and the people of the south as simply a case of geography which created not only a material division of wealth but also two distinctly different ways of life (Grant,1930). There is certainly more than an element of truth in the hypothesis that the political economy of the respective formations in the north and the south was influenced by the mainly pastoral labour relations experienced in the south and the cattle-raising economy of the north. Vulgar Marxists, for example, would argue that the essential explanatory factor lies in these fundamentally different sets of economic relations. I have tried to indicate here, however, that much more complex processes were involved, not least of which consisted of the conflict and struggle which emanated from two essentially antagonistic forces involving a primarily feudal/patriarchal set of power relations in the Lowlands and a primarily patriarchal/feudal set of power relations in the Highlands. In short, in both the Lowland and the Highland areas of Scotland at this stage, social relations consisted of a mix of feudal and patriarchal elements; whilst feudal elements were dominant in the Lowlands, in the Highlands the reverse held good.

It is within the context of this complex process of development that one of the earliest gatherings seems to have occurred. As we have seen, during the reign of Malcolm Ceann-Mor in the eleventh century, a hill-race on the Braes of Mar is believed to have taken place. It is certainly asserted that the point of origin of today's Braemar Royal Highland Gatherings was an eleventh-century incident when the King summoned the clans to the Braes of Mar, whereupon a hill-race to the summit of Craig Choinneach took place (Colquhoun and Machell, 1927; Webster, 1973). The function of this sporting practice, we are told, was to select the ablest athletes so that they might serve as postal runners for the King. While there is no eleventh-century document which specifically relates to this sporting practice, in addition to the account provided by Colquhoun and Machell presented in the introduction, the following evidence might also be considered:

1. On the hill of Creag Choineach (pronounced Kanyach) whose tree-clad precipice rises abruptly from the road leading into Braemar, Kenneth MacAlpine, first King of Scots, had his hunting seat and in the heart of the village lies unnoticed the ruins of Kindrochit Castle, the stronghold of King Malcolm (1058-1093), about whom more is known. Tradition has it that King Malcolm called the clans to the Braes of Mar to select by competition his hardiest soldiers and his fleetest messengers and this may be called, without due licence, to be the original Braemar Gatherings,(Braemar Society Unpublished Papers)

2. The Braemar Royal Highland Society was founded in 1817. But the origins of the Braemar Gatherings go back much further indeed, and for this there are two main causes. Firstly, Braemar lies in the heart of the biggest deer forest in the country and for thousands of years Kings and nobles have been drawn to the vicinity by the thrills of the chase. Secondly, its geographical position made it a point of great strategic importance in the centre of roads and tracks through the hills, leading East, North and South. It has also been, in fact, a good place for gathering, be it clan gathering, military or something more friendly. There are good reasons for believing that such meetings go back as far as the eleventh century. (Braemar: 4 July 1986)

3. When, in the eleventh Century, Malcolm Canmore King of Scotland made his decision to run a royal sports meeting on the Braes of Mar to test

out the speed and endurance of the young post runners of his Kingdom, he started something that has had a long living tradition and history in this Scotland of ours. The old castle of Kindrochit, which was the hunting lodge of King Malcolm, lies buried in the heart of Braemar, amidst weeds and rubble, unnoticed by the thousands of people who visit the village each year. It is an interesting thought that on the ground where the old Mar Castle now stands, feats of strength and endurance were attempted in the presence of the King in those far-off days and that the counterpart of that simple gathering exists in the modern Braemar Gatherings. (*Annual Book of Braemar*, 1962: p. 27)

4. Many are the tales of Malcolm Canmore. He it was who first established a system of postal runners throughout the Kingdom. At the time of this event he was resident at Braemar and one day he summoned all his tenants and subjects to meet on the mound where stands Braemar Castle. Then the King announced that he would award a magnificent baldric of gold, together with a sword and a purse of gold to the first man who could attain the summit of Craig Choinneach,(*Annual Book of Braemar*, 1962: p. 253)

In situating this event within the broader context of the policies of the Canmore Kings, the point that I wish to make is that, from the evidence available, it is quite possible to hypothesise that the policies and actions of the Canmore Kings not only led to an increased level of violent behaviour in the north, but also gave rise to the development of a network of postal runners which facilitated the process of communication. It is consistent with what is known about the Highland Gatherings to suggest that: Malcolm Ceann-Mor might have called a gathering of the clans on the Braes of Mar during the eleventh century; that a hill race to the top of Craig Choinneach might have taken place; that the function of this hill race was to select by competition the fastest athletes amongst the clansfolk in order that they might act as postal runners; and that this event is consistent with what we know about not only the point of origin of the Braemar Royal Highland Gathering but also the Highland Gatherings in general.

Hill races are certainly one of the traditional sporting practices maintained at today's Highland Gatherings. However, when considering this as a point of origin, several qualifications have to be made: (i) while tradition and popular culture suggest that this eleventh-century event might be the origin of the gatherings, the lack of original eleventh-century documentation precludes absolute certainty; and (ii) since the Highlander him/her self did not arrive until the fourteenth century, a question mark must be raised against the assertion that the hill race on Craig Choinneach was in fact a Highland Gathering of the clans and not just a gathering at which clansfolk were present. While the processes which eventually gave rise to the social differentiation between Highlanders and Lowlanders were certainly at work as early as the eleventh century, there is no evidence to support the claim that the Highlanders or the Highland clan figuration achieved a distinct identity much before the fourteenth century. All that can be said about the hill race up Craig Choinneach, and the gathering of the clans on the Braes of Mar, is that today's Highland Gatherings have developed out of a number of antecedent forms, some of which may date back to at least the eleventh century.

WILD SCOTS AND HIGHLANDERS

The term 'Highlander' was first used in the fourteenth century to describe the manners, customs and way of life of the groups of people who lived to the north of the Highland line. In terms of social organisation, the greatest distinction between the Highland and Lowland formations was the existence of the Highland clan as a distinct and powerful figuration which signified a rejection and threat to many of the anglicising and modernising forces already operating, not only in the Lowlands, but also in the south. This does not mean that clans did not exist in the Lowlands. Yet such Lowland clans as the Humes, Hamiltons and Douglas's were essentially different from the Highland clans such as the Macdonalds, Mackays or Mackintoshes. Lowland people would certainly have rejected the implication that they were clannish in the sense that the meaning of the term clannish came to be associated with a patriarchal, materially impoverished and somewhat violent way of life.

The first chronicler to use the term Highlander to describe the social differentiation of Scotland in Highland and Lowland terms is generally believed to be John Fordun. Writing in 1380 Fordun (cited in Dickinson *et al.*, 1952: Vol.1, p. 8) remarked:

The manners and customs of the Scots vary with the diversity of their speech. The people of the coast are of domestic civilised habits, trusty, patient and peaceful, devout in divine worship yet always prone to resist a wrong at the hand of their enemies. The highlanders and the people of the islands on the other hand are a savage and untamed nation, rude and independent, given to rapine, ease-loving, of a docile and warm disposition, comely in person, but unsightly in dress, hostile to the English people and language, and owing to diversity of speech, even to their own nation and exceedingly cruel.

The Highland way of life has often been depicted as the barbarous antithesis of a more civilised Lowland culture. Writing in the first half of the sixteenth century, John Major drew a distinction between the 'Wild Scots' of the Highlands and 'Householding Scots' of the Lowlands (cited in Dickinson *et al.*, 1952: Vol. 2, p. 6). Commenting on various practices, Major goes on to describe the delight which the Wild Scots take in cattle-raiding and a life of indolence. Their chiefs, he adds, largely follow bad men, are full of mutual dissension, and war rather than peace is their normal condition (cited in Dickinson *et al.* 1952: Vol. 12, p. 6). By the eighteenth century, the perception of the Highland way of life from a Lowland point of view was one of suspicion and distaste. The Highlands were seen as a dangerous and primitive periphery which was increasingly an embarrassment to the British nation. A report of the Society in Scotland for the Propagation of Christian Knowledge observed in 1748 that 'it is generally allowed that the Highlands of Scotland is not a very delightful country, nor its inhabitants the most civilised or best bred people in Europe' (Smout, 1981: p.434). The report went on to add that many of the inhabitants were wild and barbarous (Smout, 1981: p. 435). With particular reference to the Highland army which gave expression to this Highland way of life in the 1745 rebellion the *Scots Magazine* (1745: p. 51) of 1745 spoke of the Young Pretender's army as: 'made out of the barbarous corners of this country; many of whom are papists, trained up to the sword, by being practised in open robbery and violence, void of property of their own, the constant invaders of that of others; and who know no laws but the will of their leaders.'

The terms 'barbarous' and 'civilised' are themselves part of a developmental process. Social formations do not stand still but are in a continual state of flux. Furthermore, various fractions move at various rates. This process is not in any sense evolutionary in that the process at any particular period in time may be reversed. According to Elias (1987b: pp. 47), two ideas are popularly used in the concept of civilisation and its antithesis, 'barbarism'. On the one hand, the terms refer to distinctly developmental stages through which all social formations are held to move, but on the other hand it is important to remember that such concepts themselves are socially constructed by rising middle classes whose ideas of moral standards and manners are extended to include the civilising influences of the state, the constitution, and education and hence the civilising of broader sections of the population who become liberated from what is viewed as barbaric (Elias, 1987b: p.48). At the moment of its formation, the concept of civilisation was a reflection of various reformist ideas and gave expression to the way in which a rising group was able to gain access to high office and to construct a certain way of life which reproduced and maintained existing power relations. As such, the terms 'civilisation' and 'barbarism' are socially constructed and reflect nothing more than the monopolistic capacity to define what passes for behaviour within these categories.

The 1745 rebellion, of course, was ill received by the English establishment. The dominant interpretation of this period in Highland history has often been mediated by social class, religion, Lowlander and many other figurational points of reference. Even today it is sometimes claimed by aggrieved Highland scholars that Scottish children are often taught to regard the Highlander as a violent and feckless barbarian (Maclean, 1956: p. 41). It can be argued that all social formations, and not just the Highland social formation, have passed through a stage of barbarous behaviour as they have developed or moved towards a state of modernity. Furthermore, exactly which groups within the British social formation have been taught to view Highland culture as a barbarous and violent way of life may have much to do with not only those who have been in a position to write and define Highland history but also the social relations that have historically developed between the Highland and Lowland formations. An important factor in this process has been the power of the dominant Lowland figuration to marginalise and even dismiss Highland culture either as of secondary importance or as a threat to the advancement of a dominant metropolitan hegemony.

The usage of the term culture in this sense is similar to many of the high culture – low culture dichotomies which pervaded the early-1970s sociological literature on culture. As such, the same principal critique might be applied, namely that *it is incorrect to imply that one culture is superior or inferior to another and more objectively adequate to talk of two or more sets of experiences and traditions,* each culture or way of life being of equal value and yet fundamentally different. Furthermore, the distinction between Highland and Lowland ways of life has much to do with the power relations between the two social formations. *The power to define, in many cases, results from the mobilisation of political. economic and cultural resources that any particular social group can draw upon.* To understand further how this broad social differentiation developed between the fourteenth and the eighteenth centuries, it is necessary to consider some of the key characteristics of the Highland formation.

While the language of the clansfolk continued to contain a strong Gaelic emphasis, the Highland chiefs and chieftains, writes Hunter (1976: p. 7), were by the early eighteenth century equally at home conversing in French or English. The anglicisation process and the language of commerce at the Lowland cattle markets necessitated that the tribal patriarch was fluent in at least Gaelic, English and French. The increasing commercial interchange between the two societies certainly facilitated this development, but the image of the Highland chief dealing in commercial affairs through Gaelic, English and French is somewhat contradictory to the assertion that the Highlanders were in fact barbarous, uncultured and uncivilised even in the high culture – low culture frame of reference. The Highlanders in general, though, tended to be extremely superstitious. The phases of the moon were closely observed and it was only during particular periods that many utilitarian functions such as cutting turf or thatch for the houses were carried out (Martin, 1884: p. 122). Superstition was often resorted to as a means of curing illness. For what Keltie (1885: Vol. 2, p. 303) refers to as consumptive disorders, the Highlanders used to remove the fingernails and toenails of the patient, put the cuttings in a bag made from a piece of the patient's clothes, wave the bag three times around the patient's head crying, 'deis-iuil', and bury the bag in some remote place. Many historians have explained the essential differences between Highlanders and Lowlanders simply in terms of geography. Again, Keltie (1885: Vol. 1,

p. 299) explains that, having little contact with the rest of the world beyond the Highland line, the clansfolk acquired a particular character and retained or adopted many habits, customs and manners which differed widely from their Lowland neighbours. In similar vein, Stewart (1822: Vol. 1, p. 7) asserts that:

> Firmness and decision, fertility in resources, ardour in friendship and a generous enthusiasm, were the result of such a situation, such modes of life, and such habits of thought. Feeling themselves separated by nature from the rest of mankind, and distinguished by their habits, manners and dress they considered themselves the original possessors of the country and regarded the Saxons of the Lowlands as strangers and intruders.

In terms of dress, the Highlander had a very distinct Highland garb. A number of modern historians have tended to argue that the dress of the Highlander, in particular the notion of tartanry, was very much an invented tradition which emerged during the nineteenth century (Trevor-Roper, 1983). Yet there is a great deal of evidence which suggests that, while the production of clan or family tartans did not exist before the nineteenth century on such a large scale as it does today, it is in fact wrong to assert that the tartan tradition of the Highlanders was an 'invented tradition'. While the wearing of tartan may have taken on a different 'meaning' after about 1750, there are a number of quite reliable references to the wearing of Highland dress and tartan before the middle of the eighteenth century. Since so many of today's Highland Gatherings are dependent upon a symbolic tartan cultural identity, it is worth considering some of the empirical evidence concerning Highland garb. For instance, as early as 1512 John Major commented on the distinctive dress of the Highlanders: 'From the middle of their thigh to the feet they have no covering for the leg, clothing themselves with a mantle instead of an upper garment and a shirt dyed with Saffron.' (Cited in Keltie, 1885: Vol. 1, p. 326.) A Frenchman, John de Beaugue, writing about 1556 stated that: 'at the siege of Haddington in 1549 they (the Scottish army) were followed by Highlanders, and these last go almost naked; they have painted waistcoats and a sort of woollen covering variously coloured.' (Cited in Keltie, 1885: Vol. 1, p 327.)

George Buchanan, writing in his *Rerum Scoticarian Historia* of 1582, described how the Highlanders used their clothing as camouflage:

> They delight in marled clothes, especially that have long stripes of sundry colours; they love chiefly purple and blue. The predecessors used short mantles or plaids of divers colours sundry waies devided; but for most part now they are browne, more nere to the colour of the hadder; to the effect when they lie amongst the hadder the bright colour of the plaids shall not betray them .... (Cited in Keltie, 1885: Vol. 1, p. 327.)

While there is a description in many of the early accounts of various colours and dyes, there is no suggestion that these dyes formed specific clan tartans. Nor do the descriptions used here differentiate clearly between the differences in dress within the Highland formation. Perhaps one of the best descriptions on this point is to be found in Edward Burt's (1815: p. 104) letters of 1730:

> Few besides gentlemen wear the trowze, that is breeches and stockings all of one piece, and drawn on together; over this habit they wear a plaid, which is usually three yards long and two breadths wide, and the whole garb is made of chequered tartan ... The common habit of the ordinary Highlanders is far from being acceptable to the eye; with them a small part of the plaid, which is not so large as the former, is set in folds and girt round the waist, to make of it a short petticoat that reaches half way down the thigh and the rest is brought over the shoulders and then fastened before, below the neck, often with a fork, and sometimes with a bodkin or a sharpened piece of stick, so that they make pretty nearly the appearance of the poor women in London.

Again with reference to the modern Highland Gatherings it must be noted that, not only the wearing of the kilt, but also the wearing of numerous tartan symbols provides this tradition with a specific sense of Highland cultural identity. Certainly, as has been indicated here, the wearing of Highland dress and various antecedent forms of tartan help to distinguish the Highlander from the Lowlander. Yet it is important not to divorce the meaning of tartanry in all its various forms from the original context in which it developed. Furthermore, it is also important not to consider the wearing of tartan today as a completely novel development divorced from earlier traditions. While clans and tartans existed before about 1750, it is doubtful whether specific clan or family tartans were developed to the same extent as they are today with the cultural production and reproduction of so many, and in some cases mythical, symbolic family tartans. Within its original social context, a tartan or, to use the Gaelic term, 'breacon', gave expression not just to a form of dress but to a whole way of life. It is also often forgotten that, after about 1750, the wearing of the kilt and wearing of tartan never again became as popular an aspect of everyday life amongst the ordinary folks of the Highlands.

In contrast to the Highlanders, the Lowland Scots tended to be more anglicised in the sense that their language was a fusion of English and Lowland Scots dialects. In the Lowlands, too, the power of the monarchy was more effective in the sense that, just as in much of England, Lowland Scots society was primarily a social formation in which the rule of the monarchy via his/her landlords was, in principle, absolute. This contributed to a more passive way of life in comparison to that in the Highlands. As Smout (1981: p. 26) indicates, the feudal factor more that any other factor helped to differentiate the Highland from the Lowland way of life. While differences in language, superstition, dress, religion, wealth and many other social, political, economic and cultural factors contributed to the Highlander acquiring a distinctive cultural identity, one of the major contributory factors which gave rise to the Lowland assertion of 'Wild Scots' was the level of violence experienced not only within and between Highland fractions themselves, but also between Highland and Lowland fractions. Certain mediating factors such as the relative powerlessness of the king and the difficulties of stabilising the royal warrant in the Highlands have already been mentioned. There was also the Highland tradition of the creach. 'Creach' was the term given to the practice of 'lifting' cattle – from other clans, but more regularly from the Lowland Scots. In many cases, such raids involved the burning of homes, the destruction of crops and either the killing or the removal of cattle or livestock. The traditional creach is explained in some detail by Stewart (1822: p. 326): 'These predatory expeditions were more frequently directed against Lowlanders, whom the Highlanders considered as aliens and whose cattle they therefore considered as fair spoil at all times. The forays were generally executed within great secrecy and the cattle often lifted or secured for a considerable time before they were missed.'

The black cattle were the main staple product upon which the clan economy depended until the end of the eighteenth century. Black cattle provided milk, butter, meat and cheese – four of the major staple products of consumption. Their hides made shoes and clothing, while the practice of cattle droving was one of the Highlanders' major occupations during the peaceful respites from clan warfare. Yet during periods of clan feuds, cattle were often carried off by the various Highland clans. Quite often, hostile clans would initiate acts of violence by a cattle raid upon the property of another clan. As such, the practice of the creach or cattle raid provided a central tradition, not only within Highland folklore, but also Highland history.

It is not necessary to provide an in-depth account of all the incidents of conflict, struggle and violence between the Highland clans to illustrate the fact that the Highland way of life was often experienced and interpreted as violent. Table 1.1 illustrates some of the incidents of internal warfare between the clans which occurred during the sixteenth century (Macleod,1927: p. 80).

In any one instance, a number of reasons might be given as to why the Highland way of life exhibited a high rate of violence right up until the middle of the eighteenth century. In fact, there seems to be a certain degree of agreement among Highland historians concerning some of the principal reasons: (i) that the power of the king was relatively weak in the Highlands and, as a result, aggression, conflict and warfare developed at various rates between Highland fractions; (ii) that amongst the Highland clans the most violent feuds usually resulted from wounded pride or an insult to a clan member and as a result it was felt necessary to avenge the honour of the clan as a whole; (iii) that many feuds were hereditary feuds which were

Table 1.1: Internal Clan Warfare during the Sixteenth Century

Date	Clans involved
1501	The Macleans and Camerons were at war.
1501-6	Donald Dubh's insurrection was going on.
1513-19	Sir Donald of Lochalsh was in rebellion.
1528	Conflict betweeen the Macleods of Dunvegan and the Macdonalds of Sleat.
1529	A Macdonald/Maclean alliance attacked the Campbells
1539	Conflict between the Macdonalds of Sleat and the Mackenzies of Kintail.
1544	The Frazers and Clan Ranald fought the battle of Kinlock Lochy.
1545	Donald Dubh's rebellion against Queen Mary (1542-63).
1561-4	Conflict between the Macleans of Dowart and the Macdonalds of Islay.
1569	Mackintosh and Kepoch were at war.
1581	Glengarry and Kintail fell out.
1585	Conflict between the Mackintoshes and the Camerons.
1588	The Macleans attacked the MacIans.
1598	Conflict between the MacAllasters and the Macdonalds.
1599	Conflict between the Macdonalds of Sleat and the Macleods of Dunvegan.

Source: R. C. Macleod (1927: p. 80).

transmitted from generation to generation; (iv) that the strong patriarchal/ feudal relationship which bonded the clansfolk to the Highland chief meant that an insult against a clan member was invariably interpreted as an insult against the clan and ultimately the chief himself; and (v) that many clans, particularly the smaller ones, bound themselves by various treaties to larger clan units from whom they sought protection. Invariably, in order to influence the balance of power and consequently the outcome of any conflict, smaller clans were drawn into feuds instigated by larger clan units. All of these factors, and many more, mediated the rates of violence and the social arrangements and relationships that operated at any particular period or point of struggle, negotiation and conflict.

With particular reference to the modern Highland Gatherings, it is important to note that any particular creach or act of violence involving any Highland clan may have resulted from a gathering of the clan or clans. In the historical epoch when the overall clan formation was at its height, the term 'Gathering of the clan' took on a very specific meaning. The importance of mentioning this here is merely to reinforce my general point that the modern Highland Gatherings have developed out of a number of antecedent forms and traditions which existed before about 1750. The very term 'Highland Gathering' of the clan or clans during the epoch when clan organisation was the dominant structural form in the Highlands referred specifically to the practice whereby the chief or chieftains summoned the clansfolk to a gathering. Such a gathering of the clan may have been a celebration at the end of the autumn harvest, an act of council to transact clan business, or a summons for the clansfolk to gather and prepare for a creach. The 'Gathering of the clan', whether it be for a council or for a creach, was generally instigated by dispatching the fiery cross. This consisted of two pieces of wood bound together to form a cross. One of the horizontal ends was burned while the other horizontal end was adorned with a cloth dipped in blood. Symbolically this was not only a signal for the clan to gather, but it also meant that anyone who disobeyed the summons of their Highland chief or chieftain would be punished by fire and sword (Carnell, 1939: p. 162).

The carriers of the fiery cross were those athletes or runners selected by their chiefs to carry it through the clan territory. This custom is referred to on many occasions, not only within the existing literature on the Highland Gatherings but also within Highland folklore. Consider the following example:

> The carriers of the fiery cross are selected by their chiefs with great care. Indeed records show that in 1745 Lord Breadalbane's men went round Loch Tay, a distance of thirty two miles, in ten minutes under three hours ... In 1715 the fiery cross went the same round, and 500 men assembled in just two hours under the command of the Laird of Glenlyon. (*Annual Book of Braemar*, 1980: p. 173)

A second meaning which may be attributed to the pre-1750 use of the term 'Highland Gathering' arises out of the agrarian context of the Highland way of life. Such a Highland Gathering is referred to in a discussion concerning the origins of the Aboyne Highland Gatherings and Games (Aboyne, 1967: p. 19):

> 1. Behind the Gathering there is, however, a much older history ..., for it was to a great extent the custom of the Highlanders to hold an autumn Gathering in the weeks after the securing of the harvest; this ancient social tradition is one of the most characteristic features of autumn life in the Highlands ... Such gatherings gave the chiefs and chieftains an opportunity to meet and discuss business ... In addition to giving this opportunity to meet, the occasion was also appropriate for engaging in sports and healthy pastimes as well as ... the traditional dancing and music of the Highlanders.
>
> 2. In 1703 the Laird of Grant sent a summons to 600 of his people to be ready for a gathering in August. (Aboyne: 2 July 1986.)

It would be misleading and indeed incorrect to suggest that the Highland way of life necessitated a perpetual state of violence, or indeed that the pre-1750 Highland economy was totally dependent upon cattle as a staple product. Highland clans were to some extent independent, yet interdependent, self-sufficing communities. During periods of peace, the labour of the clansfolk revolved, in part, around not only the tending of cattle, but also the production of agricultural produce. Barley and oats were grown in their own fields and ground in their own querns. The butter, cheese and meat consumed by the clansfolk was the produce of their own flocks and herds. Natural beds of peat, after being cut, dried and stacked produced a supply of fuel. Linen was produced from home-grown flax, while wool from the sheep was spun and dyed with various colours derived from local plants and berries. When the weaving was finished the cloth was cleansed of oil and grease. This was done by the process of walking the cloth or the 'laughad'. Such a practice is described by Pennant (1774: p. 56): 'Twelve or fourteen women sit down on each side of a long board, ribbed lengthways, putting the cloth upon it. First they worked it backwards and forwards with their hands and then they used their feet, singing all the time.'

A number of outside accounts have mistakenly simplified the existence of the pre-1750 Highland clan way of life in terms of violence and an economic dependency upon cattle and sheep, many of which were stolen from Lowland Scots (Richards, 1982). Certainly as staple products, cattle and sheep exerted a considerable influence upon the social and economic development of the Highlands. Yet the presence of cottars and other marginal groups of people within the clan provided both a source of military power and a ready supply of manual labour. A considerable proportion of any Highland clan had only a very tenuous grip on the land. Yet while at home the clansfolk worked close to the land and developed a method of agricultural production which, because of its inefficient methods of cultivation, was heavily criticised by nineteenth-century reformers.

As Richards (1982: Vol. 1, p. 39) explains, under the 'runrig' method of cultivation the various strata within the Highland clan worked both cooperatively and individually to exploit the land in three ways: arable, fine pasture and rough grazing. At the core of this runrig practice of cultivation was the division of land into in-field and out-field pastures. The out-field land was less accessible and produced little in terms of crops. The most productive land was the in-field land which was processed under a continuous rotation of grain crops. In addition to the in-field and out-field areas, there was the common grazing land for cattle. Such a system of runrig farming has been described by one writer as a rational, integrated system adapted to the availability of resources and the agrarian context of the Highlander (Fairhust, 1967: p. 12).

This agrarian context has been mentioned here for a number of reasons: (i) to illustrate briefly that the Highland way of life before about 1750 was not, as many would have us believe, experienced as a perpetual state of violence; (ii) that while the Highland economy during this period was dependent, in part, upon such staple products as cattle, an impoverished form of agrarian subsistence also contributed to the economic development of the Highlands; and (iii) that while the evidence in most cases is fragmentary, there are indications that it was within this agrarian context that an antecedent form of Highland Gathering developed. Further examples of this practice might also include the origins of the Cowal Highland Gathering and the Trossachs Highland Gathering. While the earliest record of the Cowal gathering, in its developed form, appears in the *Argyllshire Standard* of 4 May 1894, the official history of the Cowal Highland Gathering makes reference to a much earlier form of Gathering: 'Highland Gatherings in Scotland go back many generations. It was customary for the Gaels to hold an Autumn gathering and sports prior to the "kirn" or "harvest home" when the crops had been safely gathered in.' (Cowal, unpublished papers, p. 4.)

The Trossachs Highland Gatherings claim to go back some 450 years. Local tradition has it that they were part of a celebration of the hairst kirn or bringing in of the harvest (Trossachs: 15 February 1985). Traditionally the clan Macgregor of Glengyle brought in the harvest. Such a celebration was briefly described by Percy Yorke (1821: p. 35):

> The ceremony over, the whole marshalled themselves into a line of procession, and one of the Highlanders being a piper, of which there is almost always one with every band of mountaineers who descend at harvest time to the Low Country, he headed them and struck up a 'pibroch' of triumph. On arriving at the barn door they separated and, as no work was done that day, betook themselves to various amusements to pass the interval from dinner till the hour of six o'clock, the appointed time of assembling to the Kirn-supper.

> A party of the Celts amused themselves, and me, among others, by their extraordinary feats in 'putting the stane', hopping, leaping, and running. Their agility far surpasses that of the Low Country hinds; but these in strength, if not in dexterity, are their equals. The speed with which some of them ran up the face of a hill was quite wonderful. Fiery in their tempers, they were, during their 'strives', more than once on the point of breaking out into hostilities, and their skein-dhus, a small dirk-like knife, which all Highlanders in this part of the country carry (sheathed), held up in the attitude of defiance.

While a number of cultural differences between the Highlander and Lowlander emerged between the fourteenth and the eighteenth centuries, from the standpoint of social organisation the greatest distinction between the social fractions was the existence of the Highland clan as a way of life north of the Highland line. The central axis of tension within the Highland social formation during this period resulted from the centrifugal tendencies of the Highland chiefs and a destabilising force of feudal origin. It is within a relational social context of patriarchy, feudalism and the Highland clans that further antecedent forms or today's modern Highland Gatherings may be situated.

HIGHLAND CLANS, PATRIARCHY AND FEUDALISM

> The Highlanders are divided into tribes or clans, under chiefs or chieftains, and each clan again divided into branches from the main stock, who have chieftains over them. They are subdivided into smaller branches of fifty or sixty men, who deduce their origins from particular chieftains, and rely upon them as their immediate protectors and defenders. (Burt, 1815: p. 105.)

At the apex of the Highland clan was the Highland chief whose function it was to act as leader in warfare, protector of the clansfolk, landholder and legal administrator of the clan. The most prominent members of each clan figuration, apart from the chief, were the chieftains of the various sub-sets of the parent clan. Many chieftains also held the position of 'tacksmen' and, like all chieftains, were invariably related by blood to the chief. The tacksmen generally rented or loaned land from the chief on the understanding that their principal role was to provide the chief with skilled military power rather than cash. An interesting comment is made by Hunter (1976: p. 9) when he states that the tacksmen, inordinately conscious of their status as the 'daoine waisle' or gentlemen of the clan, did not trouble themselves with the day-to-day tasks of farm labour. Instead they rented or loaned their farms to a group of sub-tenants or cottars, the latter, as sub-tenants of the sub-tenants, constituting the lowest order within this set of power relations which formed the Highland clan. For the great majority of the clansfolk, security of tenure was relatively dependent upon the good will of the chief or chieftain.

While this may have become relatively problematic during the aftermath of the Battle of Culloden, before the middle of the eighteenth century the clan as a social formation was bonded together by a dynamic patriarchal/feudal set of social relations. At the root of this Highland clan formation lay the myth that all in a given clan were descendants of a common ancestor who had in the past founded the clan. The word clan itself is, in fact, the Gaelic term for 'family' or 'children'. At the apex of this traditional power structure was the Highland chief, the senior member of the clan who, as the tribal patriarch, demanded and was often given enormous respect and loyalty from his clansfolk. This obedience and loyalty is commented upon by both Martin and Burt in their analyses of the Highlands in the eighteenth century:

> The islanders have a great respect for their chiefs and heads of tribes and they conclude grace after every meal with a petition to god for their welfare and prosperity, (Martin, 1884: p. 209.)

> The ordinary Highlanders esteem it the most sublime Degree of Virtue to love their Chief and pay him a blind obedience, although

it be in opposition to the Government, the laws of the Kingdom, or even to the law of God, (Burt, 1815 p. 105.)

The patriarchal power of the chief was derived from the principle of kinship. Personal status was given to the chief as senior member of the clan, together with the right to hold land on behalf of the clan. Hence, there was no private ownership of land. The power of the chief was not territorial in origin, but sprang from the belief that he was the natural leader or father of his people. In many cases, the patriarchal power of the chief was consolidated by a feudal charter being granted by the monarchy or some other leading powerful figure such as the Lord of the Isles. However, as Cunningham (1932) explains, the chief already occupied a position of power by natural right independently of the monarchy; the power of the Highland chief was only in the second example relatively dependent upon his social relationship with the monarchy or some other office.

Feudalism, on the other hand, rested upon an entirely different premise, in that the personal rights and the status of the landlord emerged from the ownership and control of property and land. The landlord or monarch in turn allotted land to his vassals who in turn may have allotted further portions of land to sub-vassals. Conditions of service under feudalism were often military, and when these conditions were broken the land was invariably forfeited. It was the fact of possession that upheld the landlord's right to stipulate the payment of the feu. The essential difference between the feudal and patriarchal forms of power was that one was essentially tenurial or territorial while the other was essentially personal. One was a relationship between chiefs while the other involved a broader relationship between clan chiefs and members. It is not being argued that such forms of power were exclusive to the Highlands or Lowlands; however, it can be said that a patriarchal/feudal set of relations prevailed in the Highlands, while a feudal/patriarchal set of social relations were characteristic of the Lowlands.

While stability existed in many instances where the Highland chief was also the Highland landlord, the Highlanders were in constant revolt against an anglicisation process which they identified as a direct threat to the patriarchal social relations of the Highland clan formation. A primary axis of tension developed out of feudal and patriarchal rights of marriage and inheritance. Under the patriarchal way of life, women could not succeed to the chieftainship of the Highland clan, nor could they convey the position of chief out of the clan by marriage into another clan. Moreover, under feudal practices it was perfectly feasible for women to inherit the ownership of land. An essential feature of the Highland way of life was that the Highland clan figuration was relatively dependent upon land being laid out to ensure the continued existence of the clan. However, unlike feudal forms of land ownership, the land of the Highland clan was not the private property of the chief, but the public property of the clansfolk.

It would be misleading and indeed incorrect to generalise about the

Highland social formation as being either patriarchal or feudal much before the middle of the eighteenth century. Certainly a more feudal set of practices operated more forcibly following the removal of the Highland chief's hereditary powers after the Battle of Culloden. The integration of the Highlanders after this event was but another development towards a particular form of unification. The feudal power of the Highland landlord was eventually to supersede the patriarchal power of the Highland chief. Indeed, after about 1750 many Highland chiefs rejected the old way of life and developed a different set of powers and practices as private landlords. Yet in practice, before the destruction of the Highland clan as a vital and significant focus of social organisation, what operated in the Highlands was a fusion of patriarchal and feudal forces which formed a continual axis of tension between the Highland and Lowland social formations. Both forces existed side by side in the Highlands, yet essentially in opposition to one another. When considering the effect of these forces upon the Highland social formation, I am in general agreement with the argument put forward by Smout (1981: p. 43) when he asserts that the Highland social formation was based on a kinship or patriarchal set of social relations modified by feudalism. The Lowland social formation, on the other hand, developed a feudal set of social relations modified by kinship or patriarchal considerations. Within the Highland clan figuration, rights to land were dependent upon personal status and not status upon the holding of land. The residual elements of this personal bond are still recognised in Scots law today by the fact that the Queen, in her position as monarch, is regarded as Queen of the Scots and not Queen of Scot-land.

As head of the clan, the Highland chief exercised a number of heritable jurisdictions. The existence of such hereditary powers illustrates further the fact that the Highland chiefs operated in many instances independently from the rule of the monarchy. In both civil and criminal cases the Highland chief either sat in judgement himself or appointed one of his chieftains who was in turn relatively dependent upon the Highland chief. These powers of jurisdiction are commented upon by Colonel David Stewart on a number of occasions (Stewart, 1822). For instance, the following account is given of a petition brought before the Duke of Atholl, hereditary Highland chief of the Clan Murray, in 1707 (Stewart, 1822: Vol 2, p. 51):

'My Lord, here is a petition from a poor man, whom Commissary Bissett, my baron bailie, has condemned to be hanged; and he is a clever fellow, and is strongly recommended to mercy, I am much inclined to pardon him'. 'But your Grace knows,' said the President, 'that after condemnation, no man can pardon but his majesty.' 'As to that,' replied the Duke, 'since I have the power of punishing, it is but right that I have the power to pardon'; and calling upon a servant who was in waiting, 'Go,' said he, 'send an express to Logierait, and order Donald Stewart, presently under sentence, to be instantly set at liberty.'

Just as the Highland chief in the old Highland clan formation represented a link with the past, so, too, does the position of the Highland chief at many of today's Highland Gatherings. The chieftain to the Cowal Highland Gathering and the Argyllshire Highland Gathering has always been the current Duke of Argyll. The Aboyne Highland Games are frequently run under the patronage of the Marquis of Huntly, Highland chief to the Clan Gordon. The standard of the Marquis of Huntly, chief of the Aboyne Highland Games, is always hoisted on a flagstaff at the commencement of these games (Aboyne, 1965: p. 23). The standard indicates the identity of the person in command, while the hoisting on to the flagstaff indicates the Marquis's actual presence on the field (Aboyne, 1965: p. 24). Sir John Forbes as head of the Forbes Clan is the current hereditary patron to the Lonach Highland Gathering (Lonach: 20 August 1986). Captain Farquharson of Invercauld is not only hereditary Highland chief to the Clan Farquharson, sub-set of the Clan Chattan, but also chieftain to the Braemar Highland Gathering and the Ballater Highland Games. Finally, reference might also be made to the Duke of Atholl, hereditary Highland chief to the Clan Murray and chieftain to the Atholl Highland Games. The examples here have only been cited to illustrate the point that today's Highland Gatherings are relatively dependent upon and have continued to perpetuate the cultural production and reproduction of symbols from the past in the person of the Highland chief. This is not an invented tradition but another example of the way in which today's Highland Gatherings have developed from various antecedent forms which contributed to a Highland way of life which existed prior to about 1750.

Within the pre-1750 Highland social formation, the office and responsibilities of the Highland chiefs were, in part, reflected by the figuration of clansfolk who constituted the 'Luchdtachk'. The principal members of this immediate group are listed by Logan (1876: Vol. 1, p. 8):

1. The Gille-Cowe, or henchman, who closely attended the chief and stood behind him at the table.

2. The Bladair or spokesperson.

3. The Bard.

4. The Piobaire, or piper.

5. The Gille-Piobaire, the piper's servant who carried his instrument.

6. The Gille-more, who carried the chief's broadsword.

7. The Gille-casfluich, who carried him when on foot across rivers.

8. The Gille-cambstraithainn, who led his horse along rough and dangerous paths.

9. The Gille-trusaineis, or Baggageman.

With particular reference to the modern Highland Gatherings it is important to elaborate upon the importance of the Piobaire within the clan formation. Indeed it was a poor Highland chief who could not celebrate the deeds of his clansfolk with a piper and bard as part of the 'luchdtachk'. Piobaireachd is the Gaelic word meaning simply piping, pipe music or the art of playing on the bagpipe. Research is only just beginning to lay bare some of the circumstances in which the piobaire and the piobaireachd took root and began to flourish as a folk tradition within the Highland clans (Cowan, 1980). As a cultural facet of pre-eighteenth-century clan life, the piobaire composed the piobaireachd, or pipe tune, for special or outstanding occasions to express moments of sadness and gladness in the social history of the clan. For instance, the piobaire might have provided a lament for a departed Highland chief but it might also have provided a message of loyalty and welcome to the succeeding chief. Since at least the sixteenth century, many clan chiefs and many of the chieftains have had their own hereditary pipers. It is an office kept within particular families, generation after generation. The most celebrated example of this specialisation is the MacCrummens of Skye, hereditary pipers to the Macleods of Macleod (MacAoidh, 1833). Other examples include the Macarthurs, hereditary pipers to the MacDonalds, Lords of the Isles; the Mackays, hereditary pipers to the Mackenzies of Gairloch, and the Macintyres, hereditary pipers to the Clan Menzies (MacAoidh, 1833: p. 9).

Many theorists have discussed the origins of the piobaire and the piping dynasties, especially the MacCrummens. In his account of the hereditary pipers, Aonghas MacAoidh (1833: p. 8) asserts that the first MacCrummen piper to the Clan MaCleod was Eain Odhar who in turn was succeeded by Patrick Donn, in the sixteenth century. In his personal memoirs of the Skye pipers, Angus Macpherson suggests that it was Alasdair Macleod who bestowed the lands of Boicraig on the Clan MacCrummen, whereupon the clan developed a piping school during the 1600s. Many of the pre-eighteenth-century Highland chiefs sent the piobaire to the piping school in Skye. While the MacCrummen school of piping continued into the nineteenth century, its modern counterpart can be found in the piping and dancing school of Braemar where the MacCrummen technique of bagpipe playing continues to be taught. While the Highland clans as a way of life has long since ceased to exist in its original format, one of the residual traditions maintained from the sixteenth century is that the MacCrummens of Skye still function as the hereditary pipers to the Macleods of Macleod. The development of this lineage is presented in Table 1.2 (compiled from interviews, minute books, newspapers).

It is not necessary to provide an in-depth account of the piobaire and the piobaireachd in this context. The point that is simply being made here is that as an integral part of today's Highland Gatherings, the playing of the Piobaireachd is a central tenet of the Highland tradition, albeit reproduced today in a changed and modernised form. Yet while it serves in part as a

Table 1.2: The MacCrummen Lineage, 1500-1980

Number	Name	Date
1st Hereditary Piper	Finlay a'Bhreacain	
	Ian Odhar	
2nd Hereditary Piper	Patrick Donn	
3rd Hereditary Piper	Donald Mor	1570
4th Hereditary Piper	Patrick Mor	1595-1670
5th Hereditary Piper	Patrick Og	1670
6th Hereditary Piper	Malcolm	1690
	Donald Ban	1710
	Angus Og	
7th Hereditary Piper	Ian Dubh	1730-1822
8th Hereditary Piper	Donald Ruadh	1743-1825
	Roderick	1814-80
	Malcolm	1851-1928
	Roderick Murchison	1889-1912
9th Hereditary Piper	Malcolm Roderick	1918
10th Hereditary Piper	Iain Norman	1952

Sources: Compiled from interviews, minute books, newspapers.

symbol of Highland cultural identity, it has also developed out of the tradition of the Piobaire who held an important position within the old Highland clan. Once again, all that is being said is that today's Highland Gatherings have developed out of a number of antecedent cultural forms which have their point of origin and original 'meaning' firmly rooted within the Highland clan formation. The Piobaire, the Piobaireachd and the Ceol Mor are all associated with long-standing traditions which link them to the cultural milieu of pre-1750 clan life.

Within the clan, the chieftains occupied a position of social significance which was superseded only by that of the Highland chief of the clan. The degree of power of the chieftain was mediated by his relationship to the socially superior Highland chief. It is not necessary to develop a lengthy account of the significance of the chieftain to the clan since much of what has already been said of the Highland chief applied at another level to the chieftain. The chieftain was the immediate connection that the clansfolk had with the various sub-sets of the clan. The chieftain, therefore, had a degree of power over his own clansfolk but he was dependent, in part, on the Highland chief. Like the Highland chief, the chieftain's relationship with the clansfolk was mediated through a patriarchal/feudal set of power relations. The various chieftains of the various sub-sets of a clan were not only bonded to the Highland chief through family ties; they also leased land from him. In return for the land, the chieftains ensured that the

Highland chief was provided with military support in times of feud and warfare and that the land and cattle were worked and provided for in times of peace.

It is perhaps relevant in this connection to consider one or two examples to illustrate the relationship of the chieftain(s) to the clan formation. Among the most powerful of the Highland clans were those that developed under the patronage of the Lords of the Isles during the fifteenth century. In terms of territory the Lords of the Isles controlled by far the largest and most powerful province in Scotland during the fifteenth century. At the beginning of that century it probably included all the Western Isles and such mainland territories as Kintyre, Knapdale, Morvern, Ardgour, Ardnamurchan, Moidart, Knoydart, Lochdart and Argyll. The Lordship of the Isles lasted about 150 years, finally being forfeited in 1493. As Gregory (1836: p. 59) suggests, analysis of the Highland clans which developed under the Lords indicates that they can be fruitfully divided into two broad social groups.

The first group included all those clans whose chief boasted a direct male line of descent from the Clan Macdonald. In this instance the Highland chief at any particular period of time would have been the hereditary Highland chief of the Macdonalds. However, a complex clan formation also emerged under the Clan Macdonald which included the Clan Iain Mhor of Islay, the Clan Ranald of Garmoran, the Clan Iain of Ardnamurchan, the Clan Iain Abrach of Glenco and the Clan Allaster of Kintyre (Gregory, 1836: p. 68). Each of these relatively independent clans had its own chieftains who in turn may have owed allegiance to the senior branch of the clan, namely the Clan Macdonald and their Highland chief. The second group included all those clans who were connected to the Macdonalds but not through a direct male line of descent. Included within this group were the Clan Gillean or Maclean, the Clan Macleod of Lewis, and the Clan Macleod of Harris, the Clan Chameron, the Clan Chattan, the Clan Macneil of Barra, the Clan Mackinnon, the Clan Macquarries, the Clan Macphee, the Clan Maceacherns and the Clan Mackay (Gregory, 1836: p. 68).

Many of these clans developed various branches or septs which in turn developed into relatively autonomous yet dependent clan formations. The establishment of so many relatively independent clans, comments Grant (1930: p. 491), was an early feature in the development of the Highland clan formation during the fifteenth century. Some examples of these divisions at any point between the fifteenth and eighteenth centuries might have included the Macleans of Duart and the Macleans of Lochbuy, the Macleods of Harris and the Macleods of Lewis, the Macneils of Barra, and the Macneils of Gigha, the Macdonalds of Sleat, the Macdonalds of Clanranald and the Macdonalds of Glenco. In each of these instances, the clansfolk owed allegiance in the first instance to the chieftain of their immediate branch, who in turn owed allegiance to the chief, chieftain and clansfolk of a parent branch, the members of which, in turn, owed allegiance to the

Highland chief or the closest relation to the progenitor of the clan. In all of these cases, the power of the Highland chief was mediated through his chieftains, who themselves had a degree of relative power over the clansfolk. While the action of the clansfolk might also have been further complicated, at any point in the development of the overall Highland clan formation, by monarchical bonds, in the first instance it was through the patriarchal/feudal relationship with their respective Highland chiefs and chieftains that all other actions were mediated.

Some chieftains also performed the role of tacksman. However, in general the tacksman occupied a further position within the complex webs of interdependence which developed into what became known as Highland clans. Most chiefs or chieftains leased a high proportion of their land to the tacksmen who were quite often closely related to the chief or chieftain's immediate family. The tacksman effectively organised the agricultural functioning of the clan under the runrig form of production. In general, the behaviour of the tacksmen determined the day-to-day working character of the Highland clan (Richards, 1982: p. 111). It would be wrong to assert that a private system of landownership was uniform practice much before about 1750. Certainly, some elements of this long term social process were present before this time, but the power of the Highland chief could be removed by the clansfolk if they felt that his hereditary position was being abused. Forms of private ownership began to emerge fairly early on but only became consolidated after about 1750. Prior to about 1750, the tacksmen, unless the clan was at war or organising a creach, remained on the farm. Many of the tacksmen were themselves farmers who leased tracks of land from the chief or chieftain and, in turn, sublet the land to sub-tenants or cottars. The tacksman occupied a place of high social status within the clan and, as Smout (1981: p. 316) indicates, basked warmly in the chief's reflected glory. It would be wrong to imply that the tacksmen, although farmers, actually involved themselves fully in the actual labour process. It was the sub-tenants or cottars, that is to say the lower orders in any clan, who actually worked the clan land and provided the Highland chief with a source of military power.

The actual sub-strata of the Highland clan consisted of the less powerful members of the clan who have been referred to here variously as sub-tenants, cottars and crofters. As members of the Highland clan, the sub-tenants were, as already mentioned, in most cases extremely loyal and obedient to the Highland patriarch or chief. Yet their experience of life was one of various gradations of power, inferiority and poverty. Commenting upon experiences like these, Burt (1815: p. 139) refers to the fact that the poverty of the clansfolk and the chief's patriarchal obligations to the ordinary clansfolk meant that, invariably, it became customary for the Highland chief to free the clansfolk from arrears of rent. This occurred on average about one year in every five. Life for the ordinary clansfolk was far removed from the romantic glamour that many post-1750 Lowland writers bestowed upon these sub-strata of the Highland clan. Apart from their military functions, the clansfolk provided the agricultural and pastoral labour upon which the pre-1750 clan economy depended. They paid rent to the tacksman by working his land without wages while the rest of the time was mainly devoted to procuring their own subsistence from the land. Large families, writes Smout (1981: p. 317), lived in small huts with chickens and sometimes other livestock wandering in and out. Yet it was upon these members of the figuration that the Highland chief depended not just during periods of violence but also during times of peace when the sub-tenant worked the land and performed the pastoral duties which procured whatever wealth the pre-1750 clan formation could generate.

As a complex web of interdependence, the Highland clan and the way of life associated with it continued to develop well into the middle of the eighteenth century. Immediately prior to the Battle of Culloden, which effectively brought an end to the Highland clan as a lived way of life, the power of the Highland clans can in part be illustrated by their military strength. It is reflective of the patriarchal character of Highland history that it is impossible to estimate what the total number of clansfolk was in about 1750. In particular, the documentation provides little or no evidence concerning the number of women that contributed to the power of the Highland clans. Furthermore, the only official estimate of the military power of the Highland clan is credited to Duncan Forbes of Culloden who, in 1724, transmitted to the Hanoverian government a detailed account of the Highlands and the 'manpower' of the Highland clans which were involved in the struggle against Hanoverian hegemony (Stewart, 1822: pp. 26-7). The significance of such an enumeration in the context of this discussion is merely to illustrate the strength of the clan's military power prior to Culloden and to indicate in concrete terms that a set of clans actually existed. The enumeration proceeded as shown in Table 1.3.

In this chapter I have attempted to situate the discussion of the origins of today's Highland Gatherings within the broader context of Scottish history and Highland development. The discussion has been organised around three areas: (i) the process of unification and relative anglicisation and in particular the effect which the policies of the Canmore Kings had upon the Scottish social formation; (ii) the emergence of the Highlander or Wild Scot in the fourteenth century and some of the major cultural characteristics which led to the social differentiation between the Highlander and Lowlander; and (iii) as a unique social formation within this study, the Highland clan and the patriarchal/feudal social relations which centrally bonded those involved in the Highland way of life to one another. It is a way of life which was *often misinterpreted* as being solely violent and barbarous and yet which was experienced in practice in terms of a combination of violence and impoverished material existence, and as revolving around the Highland clan-as a particular set of social relations. A central axis of tension and struggle during this stage of development derived from

Table 1.3: Clan Military Power Prior to Culloden

Clan	Number
Argyll	3 000
Breadalbane	1 000
Lochnell and other chieftains of the Campbells	1 000
Macleans	500
Maclachlans	200
Steward of Appin	300
Macdougals	200
Steward of Grandtully	300
Clan Gregor	700
Duke of Atholl	3 000
Farquharsons	500
Duke of Gordon	300
Grant of Grant	850
Mackintosh	800
Macphersons	400
Frasers	900
Grant of Glenmorriston	150
Chisholms	200
Duke of Perth	300
Seaforth	1 000
Mackenzies	1 500
Menzies	300
Rosses	500
Sutherland	2 000
Mackays	800
Sinclairs	1 100
Macdonald of Sleat	700
Macdonald of Clanronald	700
Macdonnell of Glengary	500
Macdonnell of Keppoch	300
Macdonald of Glencoe	130
Robertsons	200
Camerons	800
McKinnon	200
Macleod	700
The Duke of Montrose, Earls of Bule and Moraym, Macfarlanes, Colquhouns, McNeils of Barra, Mcnabs, McNaughtons and Lamonts	5 600
	31 930

Source: D. Stewart (1822: pp. 26-7).

the centrifugal tendencies of the Highland chiefs and a destabilising force of feudal origin.

This chapter has not attempted to provide a detailed social history of the Highland social formation but merely to contextualise and explain the origins of today's Highland Gatherings. While a great deal of empirical evidence is impossible to come by with regard to particular cultural and sporting practices, this chapter has attempted to establish the fact that an initial phase in the development of the Highland Gatherings can be located between the eleventh century and the mid-eighteenth century. During this period of development many of the cultural artefacts and customs which are so central to today's Highland Gatherings contributed towards a Highland way of life which revolved around the Highland clan. Some of these points of origin preceded the emergence of the Highlander as a distinct and recognised social category. In short, all that can be said is that a first phase in the development of the modern Highland Gathering existed from at least the eleventh century until about 1750, during which time many of the sporting traditions and cultural artefacts upon which today's Highland Gatherings are dependent existed in various antecedent forms.

2

CULTURAL TRANSFORMATION AND EMIGRATION

While an initial phase in the development of the Highland Gatherings may have existed from at least the eleventh century until about 1750, a second phase in the development of this Highland tradition lasted from about 1740 until about 1850. At least three important factors affected the development of the Highland Gatherings during this period. In the first instance, the post-Culloden policies of the British state further accelerated a process of cultural marginalisation and anglicisation which, as I have already indicated in Chapter 1 may be traced back to the eleventh century. Secondly, a number of Highland cultural practices, including sporting traditions, were transported with the *émigré*, in particular to North America. It is important not to divorce the development of these Highland Gatherings overseas from the general causes and conflicts which contributed to the emigration process during the eighteenth and nineteenth centuries whereby the descendants of those people, like the Duke of Argyll, who had been partly responsible for the destruction of the Highland culture became guardians of its existence, albeit in a romanticised form. Thirdly, in a determined attempt to retain selective aspects of Highland culture such as dance and music, many Highland Friendly Societies in Scotland and abroad actively encouraged the further development of a number of Highland Gatherings.

CULTURAL MARGINALISATION

A number of factors gave rise to the reorganisation and social upheaval that characterised much of Highland history immediately after the '45 Rebellion. An interesting, albeit crude, Marxist thesis is put forward by Burgess (1980: p. 89); he argues that the subjugation of the Highland threat was the inevitable outcome of a much longer process which emerged with the 1707 Act of Union to serve the essentially economic interests of those who had a stake in transforming Scotland into a progressive capitalist society. The logical extension of Burgess's position leads him to assert that the defeat of the Highland forces was not only inevitable, but necessary, since it was the last obstacle in the path of those who wished to encourage the recasting of the Highland social formation along capitalist lines. Taken as a whole, the argument is simply this: that the initiatives of the British state, in close alliance with Scotland's ruling class, amounted to a campaign of cultural genocide aimed at eradicating all traces of a way of life which posed a direct threat to capitalist penetration of the Highlands.

There are a number of important points of departure within the Marxist exposition put forward by Burgess. Certainly the effects of the Hanoverian government's post-Culloden policies led to a relatively increased level of dependency upon the British state. The collapse of the '45 Rebellion and the confiscation of Highland estates helped to enliven the Highland land market and increase the revenue of loyalist landowners like the Duke of Argyll (Youngson, 1973: p. 20). But to argue that this was inevitable as a result of a general process of economic determination dating back to the 1707 Act of Union is problematic. The defeat of the Highland forces may have been inevitable, but such a judgement can only be established retrospectively and other factors such as the degrees of power, the forms of military organisation and the strategies of the contending sides would also have affected the outcome. Recognition might also be given to the fact that the Highland forces almost succeeded, in the sense that they reached within about 120 miles of their target, namely, London. Finally, the question might be asked whether the strengthening of capitalist relations of production was as important as the weakening of the patriarchal association between chief and clansfolk. I would argue that it is much more realistic to assert that a fusion or interweaving of these forces contributed to an increased level of dependency upon the actions of the British state. One of the many consequences of this development was the cultural marginalisation of the traditional Highland way of life.

It is not necessary to provide a detailed account of the actual events which preceded the events of the Battle of Culloden; nor is it a central concern of this chapter to afford a lengthy discussion concerning the defeat of the Highland forces. The significance of Culloden, as I mentioned earlier, was not so much that it resulted in the defeat of the Highland forces. Rather, as Hunter (1976: p. 12) suggests, such defeats in the past had simply served as a prelude to future hostilities. What distinguishes Culloden from previous defeats is that it marked an increase in the rate at which the British state pursued its policies of cultural marginalisation designed gradually to destroy not only the Highland clan formation but also a wide range of cultural practices central to this way of life.

The legislation which most immediately transformed the Highland way of life was the Act of Proscription which took effect from August 1747. By one Act of Parliament, the British state provided the legislation which contributed to the destruction of many of the cultural traditions and ways of life which had previously existed in the Highlands. The Act banned: (i) the wearing of Highland dress; (ii) the meeting together of Highland people; (iii) the playing of the bagpipes and other forms of traditional entertainment; and (iv) the carrying of arms such as the targe, dirk, the claymore and pistols (Stewart, 1822: p. 115). Although the Act was eventually repealed in 1782, and different meanings became associated with the wearing of Highland dress, there is little evidence to suggest that the common people of the Highlands ever resumed the habit after 1747. Throughout Scotland the following words were nailed to doors of town houses and churches (Prebble, 1985: p. 311):

> And it is further enacted. That from and after the 1st August 1747 no man or boy within Scotland other than such as shall be employed as officers and soldiers in the King's forces, shall on any pretence whatsoever, wear or put on the cloaths commonly called highland cloaths, that is to say, the plaid, philebag or little kilt, trowse, shoulder belts, or any part whatsoever of what peculiarly belongs to the highland garb; and that no tartan or party coloured plaids or stuffs shall be used for great-coats, or for upper coats; and if any such persons shall, after said 1st August, wear or put on the aforesaid garments, or any part of them, every such person so offending, being convicted thereof by the mouth of one or more Justices of the Peace for the shire or stewarty, or judge ordinary of the place where such offence shall be committed, shall suffer imprisonment, without bail, during six months and no longer; and being convicted of a second offence, before the court of judiciary, or at the circuits, shall be liable to be transported to any of His Majesty's plantations beyond the sea, for seven years.

While the Act of Proscription immediately affected those cultural artefacts closely associated with many of the traditional Highland Gatherings, the Heritable Jurisdictions Act of 1747 reduced the power held for so long by the clan chiefs. The reduction in the degree of power which the Highland chief was traditionally able to exercise over his clansfolk struck right at the heart of the clan formation (Stewart, 1822: pp. 115-20). No longer could the chief marry his clansfolk, order them to take up arms or possess land in the name of the clan. When the clansfolk could no longer be legally ordered to follow their chiefs, the possibility of internecine warfare was reduced. The Highland chiefs began to be further incorporated into a Lowland way of life. Putting tradition behind them, the Highland chiefs and their subsequent descendants began to marry southern wives, send their sons and daughters to southern schools, abandon the Gaelic language and to exploit their lands commercially (S/A/S, 1831: Vol. X, p. 91). All of this they did with the encouragement of successive British governments determined to destroy the social and cultural order which had supported the Highland clan formation.

Once the chiefs lost their traditional powers, many of them lost the traditional patriarchal attachment to their clansfolk. While there were exceptions to the rule, the atrophy of the patriarchal bond between the chief and the clansfolk was generally replaced by the more purely economic bond which functioned within the landlord–tenant relationship (Prebble, 1985: p. 314). Land which the Highland chiefs had once possessed on behalf of the clan now became their land in fact and law. The relatively communal way of life of the clan was replaced by a social structure in which the power of the dominant group was, in part, materially supported by a system of land ownership. As Gray (1957: p. 11) suggests, this dominant group was composed of a handful of great landlords, old clan chiefs for whom the function of leadership of the clan had been replaced by the function of land ownership and land management. By about 1800, a mere handful of such estates had come to dominate the whole land system of the Highlands.

Partially because Highland chiefs had been used to moving both within Highland and Lowland societies prior to 1746 they made the transition to their position of power relatively smoothly. Power and social status were stratified downwards from the landlords to subordinate gentry and ultimately to the crofter or peasant. The British government was, therefore, able to pursue its policies of cultural marginalisation not by expropriating the traditional Highland aristocracy but by incorporating the more powerful members of the clan figuration within the Hanoverian hegemony (Hunter, 1976: p. 12). Only a relatively small number of Highland chiefs were exiled or executed. After the repeal of the Act of Proscription in 1782, many of the Highland chiefs-cum-landlords wore the tartan once again and kept a piper to play at their board (Prebble, 1985: p. 310). However, as has already been mentioned, at the level of popular culture there is little evidence to suggest that the clansfolk ever resumed the practice. For them such cultural artefacts belonged to the old tradition, a way of life that had been largely destroyed during the second half of the eighteenth century. By the time Walter Scott had published *Waverley* in 1814, the history of the Highlander had already begun to be not only distorted, but romanticised.

This initial discussion can briefly be summarised by saying that: (i) by the end of the eighteenth century much of the traditional clan formation had disintegrated; (ii) much of the old Highland culture and way of life had been virtually destroyed by a wave of repression after the '45 Rebellion; (iii) what emerged instead was predominantly a landlord – tenant set of social relations in which land became a source of capital gain rather than a community resource; and (iv) many of the Highland élite began to reject the old way of life and identify increasingly with a more metropolitan culture and consequently with Lowland values and norms. Such changes were merely indicators of further changes implemented by an emerging landlord class who required a greater income to maintain their status in the social circles to which they aspired. While there were many dominant moments in Highland history, few loom as large in Gaelic consciousness as the Highland clearances. It is to this issue that my attention will now be turned.

CLEARANCE AND EMIGRATION

The Highland clearances are remembered for many reasons. Most of the writing on the clearances may be crudely divided into two schools of thought. Passionate accounts have tended to concentrate on the great suffering experienced by the Highland people during the late eighteenth and early nineteenth centuries. An example of this school of thought is to be found in John Prebble's account of the Highland clearances in which the argument is simply that, after Culloden, the Highlanders were increasingly deserted and betrayed by the very people they had defended for centuries and been loyal servants to in every sense of the word. Alternatively, the dispassionate school of writers such as Bumsted (1982) and Richards (1982) have played down the degree of suffering experienced by the Highland people and tended to argue that this was but one necessary feature which characterised the agrarian transformation of the Highlands during this period. In seeking to explain what happened in the Highlands, Richards in particular argues that the landlords as much as the tenants were often victims of external influences beyond their control.

Like Richards, Bumsted makes a plea for a more rigorous interpretation of Highland history during this period. The clearances, he argues, cannot be homogenised into a conflict between coercive landlords and a passive peasantry who were unable to affect the course of their own history (Bumsted, 1982: p. 220). According to Bumsted, victimisation assumptions have clouded the analysis of Highland history and rely upon present-day, as much as historical, myth for their continuity. Yet it is debatable whether Bumsted dispels such myths entirely or merely adds to the mythology of the Highland clearances. The core thesis he puts forward is that the tenants could and did make decisions that were beyond the control of the landlords. Thus the decision to emigrate to North America and elsewhere was as much a consequence of reaction to a changing way of life as it was to eviction from the land by Highland chiefs and landlords. It was only by emigration, so the argument goes, that the Highlander could hope to hold on to the traditional way of life.

Certainly this seems to cut across the traditional or passionate view as exemplified not just by Prebble (1984) but also by Hunter (1976), in the sense that both of these accounts of the Highland clearances attempt to highlight the crofter's point of view. The primary causal factor for the suffering of the crofters is in both accounts the coercive policies of the landlords which led to the widespread replacement of the human population by sheep. They argue that the Highland landowners, in conjunction with the capitalist sheep farmers from the south, exploited Highland land and people purely in terms of profit maximisation. Undertaken for profit, the clearances were as good or bad an example of naked exploitation as has ever been seen within the British social formation. The destruction of the old Highland society was conducted with unexampled brutality and lack of concern for the tenants and other groups of people who had to scratch out a living from the peripheral edges of the Highlands. The primary determining factor in all of this was the economic and financial interests of those people whose objective it was to incorporate the Highlands into a 'progressive' capitalist formation. The Highland landowners, therefore, deliberately created a crofting or tenant community which rested upon a weak economic foundation (Dickson and Clarke, 1982: p. 151-3). When this collapsed, emigration or destruction were the stark choices facing the bulk of the Highland tenantry.

When did the clearances actually occur? Narrowly defined, the term 'clearances' generally refers to the effort of the landlords to redistribute and often reduce the tenantry living on their estates. The first clearances occurred in Perthshire during the 1760s. However, a much greater rate of eviction took place between 1780 and 1855. The people mostly affected during this period were the tenantry of Ross and Sutherland, Inverness-shire and the Hebrides (Dickson and Clarke, 1982: p. 152). A degree of overt tension and struggle between landlord and tenant continued up until the Crofters Act of 1886. As Richards (1982: p. 502) himself points out, it would be a mistake to believe that this crofting legislation brought an end to the struggle between landlord and tenant in the Highlands. If nothing else though, it did reduce the power of landlords to evict the Highland people from the land and, therefore, it can be taken to mark the end of the Highland clearances.

What major factors gave rise to this process of clearance and consequently emigration? No one single factor determined this process in Highland history. Rather, a complex interweaving of many variables and groups of people resulted in the relatively less powerful people being evicted from the land. The following are but some of the many principal factors involved. Firstly, the landlord class needed an increased level of income not only to survive, but also in order to maintain their social status within an increasingly metropolitan social milieu; secondly, the traditional staple products of cattle, agrarian subsistence and limited amount of rent provided less of a potential income than the income to be derived from sheep farming. This gave rise to the widespread replacement of the human population by sheep and, later, deer. Thirdly, the decline of the clan formation meant that the bonding between the traditional Highland chief and his followers had been weakened if not broken; fourthly, the Highland population, having been pushed on to the edges of the estate, could no longer be supported by the resources and land available; and finally, while the tenants were not powerless, they were unable to stop the effects of various modernising, forces which were changing the Highlands during these periods. These particular factors were some of the key variables associated with the Highland clearances between 1760 and about 1886.

To the Highlanders who experienced the clearing and indeed to the Highlanders of later generations, the suffering, although it was real, resulted not so much from the loss of land as from the fact that it represented an enormous betrayal of the Highlanders by their own hereditary leaders. On this point I am in agreement with the comparison made by Hunter (1981: p. 61) where he argues that it was this aspect of betrayal which marked off the Highland *émigrés* from their Irish counterparts. The Irish folk who found themselves bound for North America during the nineteenth century knew exactly who was responsible for their plight. They were the victims of a more powerful English nation, a nation whose religion, background, history, language and traditions were all quite different from the indigenous Irish culture. In contrast, the Highland *émigrés*, in many cases, were forced off the land by their own hereditary chieftains. There was hardly anything in the Highland culture which could help the *émigré* come to terms with this situation, except perhaps, as Hunter indicates, an awareness that the new order and the advent of increasing evictions, famine and poverty were experienced in much harsher terms than even the patriarchal, violent, materially impoverished clan way of life had been (Hunter, 1981: p. 62). This fact alone contributed a great deal to the idealisation and romanticisation of the old way of life.

The thesis put forward by Bumsted suggests that it was the pull to a new promised land rather than the push from the Highlands which was the critical factor behind the emigration process. The emphasis on pull factors, voluntarism and matters of agency are foremost in Bumsted's account of the Highland clearances between 1770 and 1815. Pre-1770 and post-1815 clearances are not accounted for in this particular exposition. Aside from this minor criticism, the major problem, I believe, with Bumsted's account revolves around the degree of emphasis which he places on the pull factors as opposed to the push factors. Bumsted fails to take account of the idea that a changing balance between pull and push factors may have occurred at any point within the overall process of clearance. One might conclude, in this instance, that the demise of the clan formation, with land becoming perceived as a capital rather than as a community resource, the cultural marginalisation of the Highlands along with the movement of the hereditary leaders of the clan formation into a more metropolitan culture, constant increases in rent, and increased competition for land, all appear to be critical push factors. Quite simply, the tenantry were no longer in as powerful a position to survive within the changing nexus of social relations. They either remained to struggle against greater immiseration or moved to other lands in the hope of retaining core aspects of the traditional way of life. To describe this as free choice fails to take adequate account of the notion of power and in particular of the way in which power in its relational sense structured and mediated a complex web of social arrangements. To repeat a critical statement in the text, 'only by departing his/her native land could the Highlander hope to maintain the traditional way of life' (Bumsted, 1982: p. 101). This categorically indicates that there was little option but to move, or to remain and participate in unequal conflict in terms of power and resources. If choice is significant, it primarily reflects where the Highlanders went, not the fact that they were forced to go (Fergusson, 1984).

Perhaps it is too simplistic to argue that the strengths of the work of Prebble and Hunter are the weaknesses of the work of Bumsted. Yet in refusing to accept the claims of the passionate school of writers, the interpretation of the clearances presented by Bumsted portrays the Highland tenantry as passive recipients of the forces of change. Again, a greater sensitivity to the notion of power, culture and dependency would have enabled Bumsted to provide a more complete account of the clearances in the sense that, while the tenantry were not as powerful as the emerging landlord class, they were not powerless. The absence of an adequate sensitivity to the resistance and struggle which the crofters, in particular, instigated is perhaps explained more on the basis of historical values and orientation rather than in terms of the actions of those less powerful groups of people who, while experiencing eviction, poverty, famine and congestion on the land, did not by any stretch of the imagination merely accept such changes (Dickson and Clarke, 1982: p. 168).

Consider the following examples. In 1792, 200 inhabitants of Easter Ross and Sutherland gathered to drive about 10 000 sheep from land which they viewed as being common land (Hunter, 1976: p. 94). In April 1821 Sheriff-Officers who came with Writs of Removal on behalf of Lord Stafford were literally stripped of their clothes, deprived of their papers and chased off the bounds of the property at Gruids (Prebble, 1984: p. 128). In Caithness, two women and three men were sent to Dornoch Jail for six months for obstructing and assaulting Alexander Farquhar, the messenger-at-Arms who had proceeded to read to them their orders of eviction (Prebble, 1984: p. 128). At Durness in August 1841, a Sheriff-Officer called Campbell came with the Writs of Removal, was mobbed and his papers were eventually burned (Prebble, 1984: p. 168). The Superintendent of Police at Dornoch got the same 'welcome' when he rode to Durness in an attempt to pacify the tenants (Prebble, 1984: p. 168). Two years later in Assynt, John Macleod, a small tenant at Balchladdich, stood up against the Duke of Sutherland's factor and refused to be evicted (Prebble, 1985: p. 169). While the rates of conflict and struggle might not have been as high as those which emerged during the crofters' struggle leading up to the Crofters Act of 1886, the dispassionate accounts of the clearances fail to give due recognition to the factual evidence which suggests that the crofters' resistance, however sporadic and disorganised it may have been, was in fact intense and far from passive.

A point made by Elias (1978: p. 181) in his discussion of Marx is certainly relevant to much of the historical literature on the clearances. While recognising that one of Marx's greatest contributions to sociology was to situate social class problems centrally within a theory of social development, he was unable, argues Elias, to detach himself from the idea that those social classes which were rising were all good and those which were descending were all bad. In much the same way, writers on the clearances have been unable to free themselves from the idea that all landlords were bad and all crofters were good. Some landlords, such as the Duke of Sutherland and the Duke of Arygll, were certainly responsible for mass evictions and emigration, but other landlords, such as Macleod of Dunvegan, attempted to absorb the brunt of the changes almost to the extent of ruining themselves financially. It is a central facet of this narrative to attempt to explain a process such as the Highland clearances in terms of tension and struggle between different social fractions without referring to one particular fraction as 'good' and one particular fraction as 'bad'. The argument that landlords as well as tenants were often caught up in external influences beyond their control can be made without attempting to exonerate those landlords who were responsible for exploitation, eviction, poverty and ultimately famine amongst many of the Highland tenantry. As already mentioned, to the Highlanders of later generations the horror of the people's clearances lay less in the way they were accomplished and more in the fact that they represented in many cases an enormous betrayal of groups of people by their own hereditary leaders. The patriarchal – feudal bonds which had bound the clan formation were being broken and replaced by a more economic, landlord – tenant set of social relations.

The crucial point that needs to be made in the context of this study is that the Highland clearances further contributed to a process of cultural marginalisation which not only led to the demise of the old social order but also to the less powerful people, namely the tenantry, becoming increasingly dependent upon a more powerful landlord class. The actions of the landlords continue to be controversial to this day, in the sense that the underdevelopment of the modern Highlands is in many ways one of the products of the mass evictions which took place between 1760 and about 1886. Certainly the landlords replaced previous staple products such as cattle by introducing a further staple product. The Highland economy became more dependent upon not only the actions of the landlord-class but also upon one primary staple product, namely sheep. Furthermore, the dependency and subsequent underdevelopment of the Highland social formation did not result simply from economic concerns but also from many social, political, cultural and religious actions taken by the landlords amongst others. The clearances only completed a process of cultural marginalisation which had been consolidated by the actions of the British state after the 1745 Rebellion, a process which included prohibitions against the wearing of tartan, the playing of the bagpipes and the meeting together of Highland people.

While many of the Highland landlords continued to reject the old way of life and became further incorporated with the process of anglicisation, many of the cultural traditions which contributed to the traditional Highland Gatherings were exported with the *émigré* overseas. Out of this emigration process developed many of the North American Highland Gatherings.

The first Scottish organisations formed in the United States were economic, social and cultural groups aimed at helping the *émigré*. The oldest charitable society appeared in Charleston, South Carolina, in 1729 (Donaldson, 1986: p. 24). According to the 1903 Register of Scottish Societies in the United States and the Dominion of Canada, such organisations functioned to: (i) relieve indigent *émigrés* or their families; (ii) foster and encourage a love of Scotland, its history, literature, customs (including national athletic games) and (iii) promote friendly and sociable relations amongst its members (Donaldson, 1986: p. 25). Further examples of these groupings of *émigrés* include those formed in Philadelphia in 1749, Savannah, Georgia in 1750, New York City in 1756, Albany and Schenectady in 1803 and Buffalo in 1840, to name but a few (Donaldson, 1986: p. 25). Meantime in Canada, St Andrew's Societies first appeared in 1798, and by the end of the nineteenth century such groupings existed in New Brunswick, Ontario, Quebec, British Columbia and the Northwest Territory. The first Highland Gathering in North America was probably the 1819 gathering organised by the Highland Society of Glengarry, Ontario (Donaldson, 1986: p. 26).

It is worth, at this point, keeping in mind the comment made by Gruneau (1983) in his discussion of the development of sport within the Canadian social formation. According to Gruneau (1983: p. 94), a preliminary phase of structuring the development of Canadian sporting practices involved imported and indigenous game contests, and popular recreations became increasingly subject to the limits and pressures imposed by a wide range of voluntary and municipal organisations. Canada during this early phase became to a degree dependent upon not only the sporting forms of native peoples, but also on an imported set of colonial sporting practices which were often based on oral traditions.

Certainly the Highland Gatherings might be included in a whole range of cultural practices which were both oppositional to and incorporative of North American cultural life during this period. They were oppositional in the sense that they were representative of those anglo-phonic members of a dominant group, consisting of colonial estate holders, military officers and merchants, and exploitative of not only the interests of the indigenous population but also of developing French interests. Yet Highland Gatherings were also incorporated into a way of life which, for many of the Highlanders who left the Highlands during the clearances, held a future promise of prosperity which could not and did not exist back home as a result of the social, cultural, political and economic changes that were taking place.

Among the first members of the old social order to feel the effects of the clearances were the tacksmen. Short of funds, one of the first steps that the chieftain-cum-landlord implemented was to increase the rent of this nascent middle class. It was precisely this that forced many tacksmen, unable to survive in the new order, to sell their belongings, gather a considerable number of tenants together and emigrate to North America (Creegan, 1969). Many of the tacksmen had considered much of the land to be their inheritance for past services to the chief, a feeling which gradually gave rise to resentment. As a Highland traveller noted in the 1770s, such resentment drove many to seek retreat beyond the Highlands (Pennant, 1774: Vol. 2, p. 307). As it was, the tacksmen emigrated in vast numbers in the post-Culloden decades, either directly forced out by the landlord or going of their own accord, believing that the only way to hold on to the traditional culture was to emigrate (Bumsted, 1982). Hence, many of the *émigrés* who initially left were members of the middle classes of the old clan order and, as a result of their social standing, they were different from what Smout (1981: p. 52) refers to as the ragged hosts that followed after 1815.

Increased rents, the harsh winter of 1771, and cattle blight were amongst some of the factors which contributed to some 700 Macdonalds leaving Skye for America in 1772 (Brander, 1982: p. 52). Between 1768 and 1772, some 3 000 Highlanders were estimated to have emigrated to the Cape Fear districts of North Carolina. While other Scots also emigrated to North Carolina, it was particularly Highlanders who settled in the Cape Fear districts where they tended to form distinct cultural groupings, retaining their own language and garb and, in many instances failing to integrate with other settlers (Brander, 1982: p. 55). Another harsh winter, that of 1783, saw famine barely staved off in the Highlands as a result of the distribution of relief. The familiar complaints of rising rents, uncertainty of tenure, poverty and disaffection with a changing social formation convinced many Highlanders that the only course open to them was emigration. It was no longer just the tacksmen who were leading large parties abroad but also ministers, priests, and in some cases, Highland chieftains who were unable to survive in the new order (Brander, 1982: p. 60).

Table 2.1: Migration of Highland and Lowland Scots to British North America, 1760-1815

Period	British N. America	Thirteen Colonies	Highland	Lowland	Unknown
1763-75	1 143	20 000	11 043	10 000	
1776-89	1 080	1 000	1 480	600	
1790-3	1 771	1 000	2 271	500	
1794-1800	160	no data	14	143	
1801-3	7 100	1 000	7 000	1 100	
1804-15	3 400	no data	2 500	500	400

Source: J. Bumsted (1982: p. 299).

While the degree of emphasis which Bumsted (1982) places on the pull factors to North America might be questionable, the empirical data provided in his text provide a useful insight into the number of Highlanders who emigrated to British North America between 1760 and 1815.

Whatever the explanation for this emigration of Highlanders to North America, it is clear that a vast number of Highlanders, unable to survive in the changing social formation of the Highlands, did in fact leave that region. This process of emigration has continued through to the present day. The choice facing Highlanders during the late eighteenth and early nineteenth centuries was to remain in the face of changing cultural, economic, social and political pressures or to emigrate in an attempt, not just to survive but also to hold on to a traditional way of life which had become marginalised in its original context. Those who remained continued to be locked into the increasingly unequal conflict between landlord and tenant, a form of tension which in a residual sense contributed to the Crofters War which secured the Crofters Act of 1886. Those who left took with them many of the cultural artefacts and traditions which subsequently contributed to the emergence of a vast number of Highland Gatherings in North America at a much later date. Some of the following are examples of the earliest Highland Gatherings formed in Canada and North America.

Although the Glengarry Highland Society Gathering of 1819 is probably one of the earliest Highland Gatherings organised in Canada, the oldest continuous Highland Games are those sponsored by the Antigonish Highland Society founded in 1816 (Donaldson, 1986: p. 26). The first games took place in 1863. By 1867, Scottish Highland Gatherings and Games had spread across the whole of Canada. In much the same way, Caledonian Highland Gatherings were instituted in Boston, New York City, Philadelphia and Newark, New Jersey by the end of the nineteenth century. Highland dancing, bagpipe music, athletic events, tartan-costumed chiefs, *émigré* clansfolk, and prizes for the best dressed Highlander were all common practices at these early Highland Gatherings and Games. An interesting comment is made by Donaldson (1986: p. 27) when she states that the Highland Games held by the New York Highland Society of 1836 represented an early culling of nostalgic pride among *émigré* Scots – a form of behaviour which, as I shall argue later, contributed to a romantic view of the Highlander divorced from the original, and to a certain extent continuing, social context of dependency and underdevelopment experienced in the Highlands.

Founded in 1853, the Boston Caledonia Club held its inaugural Highland Games that same year. The Boston Scottish Club advertised its tenth annual Highland Games in 1866, the same year as it merged with the Boston Caledonia Club (Scottish American Journal: 11 August 1866). Thereafter known as the Boston Caledonian Club, the organisation continued to sponsor Highland Games well into the twentieth century. The objectives of the Club as laid down in Article I of the Club's constitution included the following statement:

Whereas physical culture is considered by all in our day to be an essential element in the education of young men, in order to qualify them for the more important duties of active life; and believing that no physical exercise conduces more to a perfect physical development than the Scottish national games; and knowing, also, that the practice of these games fosters and keeps alive the associations, social customs, and the memory of the land of our fathers' birth; therefore we, the members of the Caledonian Club of Boston, for our better physical and mental improvement, do hereby agree to the following Constitution, Bye-Laws, and Rules of Order. (Cited in Donaldson, 1986: p. 28.)

Another example might include the San Francisco Highland Games which date back to 14 November, 1866. Like many other *émigré* Highland Societies, the objectives of the Society included the encouragement and practice of highland games; the preservation of the customs and manners of Scotland; the promotion of a taste for the Gaelic language and literature; and the binding more closely of the social links amongst sons and daughters and general descendants of *émigrés* (Donaldson, 1986: p. 32). By 1867, the San Francisco Highland Games had instituted the tradition of the chief's message. That year, Donald Maclennan addressed the assembly with the following words:

We are assembled here this morning to participate in the sports so dear in the memories of our native land. Though transplanted, as it were, to the shores of the Pacific many thousands of miles from bonnie Scotland, still the hearts of her children warm at the recollections of their youth, and beat more strongly at the mention of her name. It has been one of the peculiarities and the pride of our people, in whatever portion of the globe we may dwell, to honor and cherish all that reminds us of our earlier years; and in *those fond recollections* we harbor our national Games, to celebrate which we are met here today. (Donaldson, 1986: p. 33)

It is not necessary to provide example after example to illustrate the point that, by the time the North America United Caledonian Association was formed towards the end of the nineteenth century, Scottish Highland Games had been firmly established as forms of sporting practice within North America. The term 'North America' is deliberately used in the sense that the *émigrés* did not form two separate national associations, one in Canada and one in the United States. Indeed, as Redmond (1982: p. 11) has indicated, the importance of the *émigrés'* cultural identity as Scots took precedence over any Canadian or American national identity during this period. Yet it was a cultural identity which was already beginning to be transformed, mythologised and romanticised. It is doubtful, if history is remembered, that these first *émigrés* who experienced the changing way of life, the poverty, famine and evictions of the Highland clearances would have shared the same 'fond recollections' expressed in Donald Maclennan's speech at the 1867 San Francisco Highland Games. Indeed, if one uses the example of another Maclennan, namely Hugh Mclennan, a leading exponent of Canadian national identity, it was more an expression of relief that he experienced when he returned to Montreal from the empty glens of Kintail (Hunter, 1981: p. 61). The North American social formation, unlike the Highland social formation, had during the nineteenth century a prosperous future in which many *émigrés* were involved. In North America there was no anti-landlord ideology or movement and, despite the fact that many *émigrés* experienced discrimination in both Canada and America, it did not take place within the same sort of social context as the crofters' struggle which was being experienced back in the Highlands. Indeed, there was a growing climate of optimism in North America.

In short, the experience of the Highland *émigrés*, and ultimately their view of the Highlands and Scotland as a whole, were radically disconnected from reality. As older cultural and linguistic links with the Highlands gradually disappeared, mythology and romance came more and more to encapsulate this picture of life in the Highlands. The dominant interpretation of Highland history became one in which clansfolk were expelled because of their bonds of loyalty to the Stuart monarchy. Such an interpretation fails to take account of those Highland chiefs who became landlords and stood to gain financially from the emigration of the less powerful members of the Highland social formation. Nor does it take account of the process of cultural marginalisation or indeed the conflict between landlord and tenant or clansfolk and chief. Yet it was not just in North America that the image of the Highland way of life and indeed of the Highlander was being transformed and romanticised.

CULTURAL TRANSFORMATION

The Highland Societies of Scotland emerged during the late eighteenth and early nineteenth centuries in response to the widespread destruction of Highland culture after the '45 Rebellion. Some of these early Highland and Friendly Societies promoted the development of a number of Highland Gatherings and Games. Lonach and Braemar are but two of the most notable examples. Following the repeal of the Act of Proscription in 1782, the wearing of Highland dress became popular among, not just the Highlands social élites, but in particular also among their Lowland counterparts. Although the kilt was sometimes worn by the Highland landlords for everyday purposes, it generally became a ceremonial form of dress (Grant, 1961: p. 326). Amongst this social élite, the practice of wearing the kilt and other forms of tartanry had been greatly influenced by the romantic novels of Walter Scott. The revival of interest in Highland culture contributed to the visit of George IV, in full Highland dress, to

Edinburgh in 1822, an act which itself was designed to further foster the incorporation of Scotland into the emerging British hegemony (Grant, 1961: p. 261).

It should not be forgotten that, while the romantic storybook picture of the glens of the Lowlands and the south of Scotland was just beginning to catch on, the real glens of the north were still being emptied as Highland people were evicted from the land, migrating to the Lowlands and emigrating to North America. The Highland Societies, in fact, did a lot not only to foster Highland sentiments but also to facilitate the process of emigration. Such societies as the ones formed in London in 1778 and in Edinburgh in 1780 did a certain amount as far as the preservation of piping skills and the encouragement to wear Highland dress were concerned, but a paradoxical situation also emerged in which many of the descendants of those people who had been responsible for the destruction of the old Highland social order were now becoming the guardians and promoters of both Highland culture and of Scottish cultural identity in general. Having first mythologised the Highlander as a threat to Hanoverian hegemony and the progressive forces of capitalism, the symbolic artefacts of the Highlander such as the kilt, tartan, dirks and sporrans now came to be regarded as the crucial symbols not of a specifically Highland cultural identity but of Scottish cultural identity as a whole. The Highland Societies themselves were small groups of people who, in general, supported and facilitated the conditions of dependency that were being created in the Highland social formation with all the resultant consequences of emigration, sheep farming and crofting.

Many of these Highland Societies were socially exclusive in that they functioned in many instances to facilitate the interweaving between members of the social élite in the Highlands and the overall Scottish social formation. As already mentioned in the introduction, the Northern Meeting of the Inverness Society was formed on 11 June 1788 (Minutes, Northern Meeting: 11 June 1788). As the minutes of the first meeting indicate, military personnel were well represented on the organising committee, with Colonel Hugh Grant of Moy, Captain Alexander Mackenzie, Captain William Wilson, Captain Gregory Grant and Lieutenant John Ross. The Duke and Duchess of Gordon, Lord Huntly and the Earl of Seaforth were amongst some of the many landlords and ladies who regularly attended the social functions of the Inverness Society. While Highland Games did not figure in the proceedings of the Inverness Gathering until 1840, the minutes indicate that dances and elaborate balls were held annually: 'That an Annual Meeting of Gentlemen, Ladies, and their Families, shall hold in this place for the Space of One Week, to commence on the last Monday of October First, and thereafter on the last Monday of October Yearly, and that for the Purpose of promoting a social intercorse.' (Minutes, Northern Meeting: 11 June 1788.)

On 23 June 1815, the *Inverness Journal* reported that at a meeting earlier that month a number of Highland gentlemen had formed themselves into a 'pure' Highland Society in support of dress, language, music and characteristics 'of our illustrious and ancient race in the Highland and Isles of Scotland'. Membership of the Society would certainly not have included the Highlanders of Kildonan who that same month had emigrated to Canada only two years after the anti-clearance riots of 1813 had taken place in Kildonan and Assynt (Richards, 1982: p. 299). This was an exclusive Highland Society for those Anglicised gentlemen and ladies of the Highlands who owned land (Prebble, 1984: p. 143). Alistair Ranaldson, an early President of The Society of True Highlanders and befriended by Walter Scott, was despised by Robert Burns because of his 'arrogance and indifference to the true condition of the Highland people' (Prebble, 1984: p. 144).

The origins of the Braemar Royal Highland Society are slightly atypical in that the Society takes its point of origin from a meeting of the Braemar Wrights Society which took place in January 1816 (Braemar: 4 July 1986). As was noted earlier, the early social composition of this society consisted not of the local landed gentry but primarily of local skilled manual workers, mostly carpenters, who developed the society as a form of collective social insurance in the absence of any welfare state. It could also be said to have been an early form of trade union and, as such, carried kinship and friendship a practical step further by organising social relief in times of hardship for the sick, the elderly, the widows and orphans among its membership. Yet from these origins at the level of popular culture, by 1826 the Society had been transformed into the Braemar Highland Society. While social relief remained one of the membership functions, other primary tasks included the preservation of the kilt, language and cultural interests of the Highlands (Jarvie, 1986: p. 351). By 1831, the vice-presidents of the Braemar Highland Society included Lord Elcho, Sir David Kinlock, Sir Thomas Lauder, and Sir William Cumming, all titled landowners (Jarvie, 1986: p. 351). In 1832 another landowner, the Marquis of Caermarthen, presented each of his gamekeepers with a complete Highland costume of his own prefabricated Dunblane tartan. That same year, the society included athletic contests in its Gathering for the first time.

By 1832 the Lonach Highland and Friendly Society had formed. The inaugural meeting of this Society is commented upon by one of the original committee as follows:

> Although the games did not start until the 1830s, the actual Society was formed in 1823 ... The Society was spoken about in 1822 at the coming of age of John Forbes who is the older son of Sir Charles Forbes the first Baronet of Newe ... They were having a bonfire at his coming of age on the top of the Lonach hill on the 15th December 1822 and they decided then that they would form the Society. (Lonach: 20 August 1986.)

The residual elements of the clans Forbes, Wallace and Gordon, have formed a strong connection with the Lonach Highlanders. Like many of the Highland Societies, the objectives of the Lonach Highland and Friendly Societies are fourfold: (i) the preservation of Highland garb; (ii) the support of loyal, peaceable, upright and manly conduct; (iii) the promotion of social and friendly feelings amongst the inhabitants of the district; and (iv) establishing a voluntary fund from members with the proceeds being directed towards social relief amongst members of their families (Lonach: 20 August 1986). While the facts alone indicate that the Highland Societies contributed to and supported the emigration process, it should also be noted that, in contrast to many of the modern Highland Gatherings and Games, it is at the Highland Gatherings of such Friendly Societies as Lonach, Braemar and Glenisla that glimpses of some of the residual elements of the past may be seen. Yet even here an idealised image of feudal bonding with the landlord is portrayed through a blending of romantic kitsch symbols with the residual symbols of the past; such a romantic cultural transformation was in no small part due to the writings of Walter Scott.

A revival, not just in the wearing of the kilt and plaid but also in the fashion of tartanry in general, had developed by the time King George IV visited Edinburgh in 1822. The following account is given of one of the social engagements attended by the monarch (Grant, 1898: p. 261): 'a great mistake was made by the stage managers – one that offended all the southern Scots; the King wore at the levee the Highland dress. I dare say he thought that country all Highland, expected no fertile plains, and did not know the difference between the Saxon and the Celt.'

After George IV had visited Scotland in 1822, Messrs J. Spittal and Son of Edinburgh wrote to William Wilson and Son of Bannockburn saying 'we are likely to be torn to pieces for tartan, the demand is so great we cannot supply our customers' (Grant, 1898: p. 262). While the fashion of wearing tartan partly resulted from the royal seal of approval being given to this and other symbols of Highland culture, much of the revival was also connected with the influence of the Scottish enlightenment and in particular with the romantic images of the Highlander presented by Scott in *Waverley* (1814) and other novels. Consider the following extracts from *Waverley*:

> He was an old smoke-dried Highlander wearing a venerable grey beard and having for his sole garment a tartan frock, the skirts of which descended to the knee. (Scott, 1814: p. 192)

> It was up the course of this last stream that Waverley, like a knight of romance, was conducted by the fair Highland damsel, his silent guide. (Scott, 1814: p. 76.)

> In the progress of their return to the castle, the chieftain warmly pressed Waverley to remain but for a week or two, in order to see a grand hunting party, in which he and some other Highland gentle-

men proposed to join. The charms of melody and beauty were too strongly impressed in Edward's breast to permit his declining an invitation so pleasing. It was agreed, therefore, that he should write a note to the Baron of Bradwardine expressing his intention to stay a fortnight at Glennaquich. (Scott, 1814: p. 184.)

In *Waverley* (1814) the main heroes are an inexperienced Hanoverian officer, who ultimately fights for Charles Edward Stuart, a loyal Hanoverian officer who fights against him, a very old-fashioned Lowland baron and a hot-blooded Highland chief who repeatedly steals Lowland cows. Like many other of Scott's novels, a peculiar mixture of fact and fiction provides a romantic historical novel which as Lukàcs (1975) observes, is also dependent upon enlightenment realism. By this he means that Scott identified with the past only in the sense that it no longer posed a threat to the established order. The romanticism of Scott, and others, was based on the belief that the past was really gone and that past history should not be used as a basis for social or political mobilisation (Nairn, 1981: p. 115). Consequently, the Highland images presented by Scott are not those of eviction, poverty, famine and increasing dependency on the landlords but ones of tartan kilts, ben and glen romanticism and the kilted Borderer. Believing that the past was not linked to the present, Scott welcomed George IV to Edinburgh in the early nineteenth century.

In Scottish terms, it is certainly arguable that the collapse of a distinctly Highland way of life after the failure of the '45 Rebellion gave rise to a process of cultural marginalisation and subsequently a process of cultural transformation. The Highlander was rendered safe to be assimilated into the imagination of the Lowland Scot and the Scottish way of life in general. A culture was by and large destroyed after Culloden and yet, precisely because of this, its symbols became available not only to a nascent European Romantic movement, of which Scott was part, but also to Scottish cultural identity in general. Because of the obscurity of Highland history and because of the popular tide of feeling at the time towards the Highlanders, the literati had relatively few problems in locating a sentimental Scottish nationalism north of the Highland line. What is of concern here, though, is not so much the influence of writers such as Scott within the European context, but rather the legacy which was left for the Highlands after its culture had been marginalised and transformed. It was left with images of purple hills, monarchs of the glen, romantic heroes and kilts, tartans, claymores and other Highland symbols, all of which were adopted as images of the real Scotland. Forgotten were the realities of the clearances, what the '45 Rebellion actually stood for and the experiences of famine, poverty and eviction.

The period between about 1740 and about 1850 marked a very distinctive stage in the development of the Highland Gatherings. It was a stage during which the Highland Gatherings, like many other aspects of Highland culture, were influenced by the British state's post-Culloden policies. An initial phase of cultural marginalisation was subsequently followed by the Highland clearances and emigration, in particular to North America. The people who remained became increasingly dependent upon the actions of the Highland landlords, many of whom had been Highland chiefs within the old clan formation. The process of emigration contributed to the emergence of Highland Gatherings and Societies overseas. In Scotland, the paradoxical situation developed by the early part of the nineteenth century whereby many of the descendants of those landlords who had contributed to the demise of the Highland way of life became the guardians of its existence. Many of the graphic symbols which were adopted by the Highland and Friendly Societies became romanticised and in part divorced from their original social context. The romantic images produced by Walter Scott and other writers certainly contributed to this process of cultural transformation. It was a transformation which was to contribute, not only to the emergence of the 'sporting landlord' phenomenon but also to the processes of 'Balmoralisation' and the popularisation of the Highland Gatherings.

3

THE SPORTING LANDLORDS

It cannot be argued that there was a direct monocausal link between the financial difficulties of sheep farming and the development of the Highlands as a sporting playground during the Victorian period. However, the decline in the fortunes of sheep farming, the increasing wealth of the metropolitan sectors of capital, the influence of not only the traditional aristocracy but also of the *nouveaux riches*, the further entanglement of land ownership with financial capital and an improved network of communication were certainly some of the key structural factors which contributed to the process whereby the Highlands became increasingly dependent upon the sporting landlords of the late nineteenth century. In a relational sense, the power of those at the apex of the Highland formation to implement cultural, political and economic changes had an immense effect upon the way of life experienced by the small tenantry or crofting class. While those people who worked the land were not powerless, they were not as powerful as the dominant grouping of this period, namely the sporting landlords. They were locked, in short, in a relationship of what one might call heavily asymmetrical interdependence.

The power of the sporting landlords to control and influence the agenda led, in part, not only to the popularisation of the Highland Gatherings and Games but also to a process of increasing cultural dependency whereby the images and practices associated with this sporting form continued to be selected, romanticised and attributed different meanings. Two crucial developments which took place between about 1840 and about 1920 were: (i) the process of 'Balmoralisation', whereby the Scottish Highland Gatherings became inextricably linked with 'Balmorality', loyalty and royalty; and (ii) a popularisation process involving the popularisation of both the Highland Gatherings and of the Highlands as a sporting playground. These developments took place against a background of tensions and struggles between two broad interdependent social fractions, each with a greater or lesser degree of power. On the one hand there were the landowners who paraded as Highland chiefs at the Highland Gatherings, and who continued to facilitate the emigration process and converted many of the nineteenth-century sheep farms into deer forests for sporting purposes. In contrast to the way of life experienced by the sporting landlord class, the crofters, those who were primarily responsible for working the land, experienced on the other hand poverty, famine and land congestion during the Victorian period.

The passing of the Crofters Act of 1886 marked an important milestone in Highland social development. The demand for crofting legislation followed the Napier Commission's inquiry into the living conditions of the Highland crofters during the early 1880s. By recognising the crofting community's claim to security of tenure and independently assessed rents, the Act brought to an end, by and large, an intensive period of eviction, oppression and exploitation which followed the defeat of the Highland forces at Culloden. While the Crofters Act managed to provide the crofters with a degree of power in relation to the sporting landlords of the nineteenth century, it failed to return the ownership of land to the direct descendants of the clansfolk of a previous epoch. The end of one period of struggle marked the beginning of another.

BALMORALITY AND THE GLAMOUR OF BACKWARDNESS

The future of the crofters during the 1840s, according to Hunter (1976), was as bleak as it could be. Poverty, threat of eviction, overcrowding on the peripheral allotments of land and a yawning chasm between income produced and rent paid to the landlord were some of the crucial facts of life which structured crofting experiences. Such experiences of hardship and hunger were exacerbated by the failure of the staple product of the crofting communities, namely the potato. Commenting upon the dependency of the crofters upon this staple product, the Minister of Morven wrote that the potato root was the crofting population's staff of life (Hunter, 1976: p. 28). While the losses were greatest amongst the inhabitants of the Western Isles, no area of the Highlands escaped the potato famine which began after about 1846 and continued to the early 1850s. The Highland *émigrés* of previous years were soon to be joined by more of their compatriots who were forced to leave the land through experiences of starvation and eviction. Specifically, they experienced starvation when the staple product of the crofting community failed, and eviction followed owing to the lack of income to pay the rent demanded by the landlord.

In stark contrast to the experiences of the crofters, other developments in the Highlands during the first half of the nineteenth century gave rise to the emergence of the sporting landlords, a class of people whose pursuit of pleasure and material wealth resulted in the transformation of many of the sheep farms into deer forests for stalking and shooting purposes(Hawker, 1893). Of course, the two sets of crofting and landlord experiences were not in a causal sense totally divorced from each other. The drop in income which the landlords experienced as a result of the potato famine certainly encouraged the landlord class to find supplementary forms of income. As yet, the decline in the fortunes of Highland sheep farming was only one relatively major factor affecting the development of deer forests. As sheep walks declined, the deer forests expanded reaching 3 599 744 acres by 1912, one fifth of the Scottish land area. Yet the potential of the Highlands as a sporting domain had already been recognised. As early as 1833 the Earl of Malmesbury offered sporting rights on the island of Harris for £25 (Jarvie, 1986b: p. 50). That same year another writer wrote (Barron, 1907: Vol. 2, p. xxxvi):): 'This was the first year that the Highlands became the rage, deer forests were made and rented for prices not exceeding £300 ... at that time a stranger could shoot over almost any part of the Highlands without interruption. The letting of the farae naturae being unknown to their predecessors.'

About this time, according to Malmesbury, the Highlands began to develop as one of the sporting and recreation domains, in particular of the southern aristocracy (Barron, 1907: Vol. 2, p. xxxvi). The evidence provided by Malmesbury above refers not only to an approximate date and an approximate cost of renting deer forests, but also to an antecedent ideology which operated in the Highlands, namely that at one time the Highlands were relatively open to any stranger who wanted to shoot deer. The letting of land for shooting purposes had been unknown prior to this period. More specifically, Malmesbury does in fact reinforce a residual ideology, one which is no longer dominant, that pertained in the Highlands, namely that the land and its contents belonged to the clansfolk and not the landowners. Certainly the shooting of deer in the Highlands existed long before this period, but what marked the Victorian epoch from the past was the systematic development of deer forests as private sporting estates and the subsequent profit for some.

It was against the historical background of contrasting crofting and landlord experiences that the Balmoralisation process occurred. Between the 1840s and early 1900s, Queen Victoria resided on Deeside, in the first instance as a tourist and in the second instance as a landowner and chieftain to the Braemar Royal Highland Gatherings (McConnachie, 1895). The patronage bestowed on the Braemar Royal Highland Gathering by Queen Victoria marked the beginning of a Balmoralisation process which linked together a bonding between the reigning monarchy, the Balmoral estate and the Braemar Royal Highland Gathering in particular, although not exclusively. This process contributed greatly to the cultural production and reproduction of the Highland Gatherings in a particular social form. It was a form or set of practices which in no small way became characterised in terms of loyalty, royalty, tartanry and Balmorality. The Balmoralisation process was closely linked to a second process of popularisation which involved not only the popularisation of the Highland Gatherings and Highland Games but also the popular development of the Highlands as a sporting playground for a certain social élite. The two processes of Balmoralisation and popularisation were inextricably linked – historically, socially and politically.

It was the prospect of shooting deer that first attracted royalty to the Highlands. The development of sporting estates received royal approval with the visit of Prince Albert and Queen Victoria to Drummond Castle in 1842 (Duff-Hart Davies, 1978: p. 101). The couple returned to the Highlands in 1844 visiting the estates of Ardeverikie and Glenlyon (Barron, 1907: Vol. 3, p. 57). Initially this sporting practice was primarily a male preserve. For instance, the *Inverness Courier* of 19 August 1849 refers to the Marquess of Douro shooting at Achnacarry, Lord Ward shooting at Glengarry, Lord Macdonald and Captain Turner at Castle Leod, Lord Selkirk at Upper Morar and Lord Lauderdale shooting on the Lochbroom estate. Yet the involvement of Queen Victoria (1838-1901) in this sporting form encouraged further female members of the aristocracy to participate in a sport which had hitherto remained patriarchal and almost exclusively characterised as a male preserve. While increased participation rates by female members of the aristocracy failed to give rise to any form of equal opportunity within the sport either in terms of gender or class control, nevertheless the involvement of such female members of the aristocracy as Lady Seymour, who stalked the deer at Achnacarry in 1845, and Lady Meux, who stalked the deer at Ceannacroc in 1857, might be cited as examples of increasing participation by women in this particular, exclusive form of sporting practice (McConnachie, 1895: p 237). Within the sporting landlord class the involvement of women represented both a development and challenge within male upper-class leisure forms.

The diaries of Queen Victoria are full of insights into the development of her close affinity with the Highlands. Here I have selected only two extracts to add weight to the evidence that such a development had taken place prior to 1848:

> There were a number of Lord Breadalbane's Highlanders, all in Campbell tartan, drawn up in front of the house, with Lord Breadalbane himself in Highland dress at their head, a few of Sir Neil Menzies men, a number of pipers playing, and a company of 92nd Highlanders also in kilts. The firing of guns, the cheering of the great crowd, the picturesqueness of the dresses, the beauty of the surrounding country, with its rich background of wooded hills, altogether formed one of the finest scenes imaginable. It seemed as if the great chieftain in olden feudal times was receiving his sovereign. It was princely and romantic. (Victoria, *Diaries*: 7 September 1842.)

> The English coast appeared terribly flat. Lord Aberdeen was quite touched when I told him I was so attached to the dear dear Highlands and missed the fine hills so much. There is a great peculiarity about the Highlands and the Highlanders; and they are such a chivalrous, fine, active people. Our stay amongst them was delightful. Independently of the beautiful scenery, there was quiet, a retirement, a wilderness, a liberty and solitude that has a charm for us. (Victoria, *Diaries*: 3 October 1844).

The evidence provided may be drawn upon to make several points: (i) that the monarchy had already established a close connection, a bonding of affinity with the Highlands during the early 1840s; (ii) that by this time the wearing of family tartans had become a fashionable tradition amongst the Highland landlords, one that was given royal approval; (iii) that the image of Highlanders in the eyes of the southern aristocracy had dramatically changed in a relatively short period of time from being barbarous, threatening and hostile to being fine, chivalrous, active people. Now that the Highlander no longer posed a threat to the established order, the ideology and rhetoric attributed to him/her quickly changed; and (iv) that the way of life experienced by royalty and the aristocracy was certainly materially worlds apart from the way of life experienced by the majority of the Highland population during this period.

By the time the monarchy had acquired the Balmoral estate in 1848, a number of new sporting estates had emerged. The Marquess of Salisbury purchased the Island of Rhum in 1845 specifically to furnish himself with a deer forest (Barron, 1907: Vol. 3, p. 135). Three years earlier Edward Ellice had bought Glenquoich for £32 000 (Mitchell, 1893: Vol. 1, p. 79). So popular had forests and moors become that the *Inverness Courier* of 19 August 1840 reported that many sportsmen had to return south after travelling the whole of the north in search of shooting quarters without being able to 'obtain a nook or cranny'. The major sporting estates developed in the 1840s included Jura, Rothiemurchus, Kinlochewe, Ardverikie, Glencalvie, Glenquorch, Patt, Flowerdale and Altournie (Orr, 1982: p. 169). In 1846 Robert Somers commented that, if the sporting forests were to increase over the next quarter of a century as they had done over the last quarter, then 'the Gael will perish from their native soil' (Somers, 1877: Letter No. 25).

The Balmoral estate at one time belonged to the Earl of Mar, who was succeeded by the Gordons. In the seventeenth century, the Marquess of Huntly, chief of the Clan Gordon, sold part of the estate to the Farquharsons of Invercauld (McConnachie, 1895: p. 237). By 1746 the estate had passed into the hands of the Farquharsons of Auchendryne and Inverey who in turn sold the estate to the Earl of Fife in 1748. The Earl of Fife, after leasing the estate to Sir Robert Gordon, subsequently leased it to Prince Albert in 1848. The new owners of the Balmoral estate arrived on 8 September 1848. Commenting upon the occasion, Queen Victoria noted in her *Scottish Diaries* (1868: 8 September 1848): 'We arrived at Balmoral at a quarter to three. We lunched almost immediately and at half past four we walked out and went up to the wooded hill opposite the windows ... The view from here looking down upon the house is charming. To the left you look towards the beautiful hills surrounding Loch-na-gar, and to the right towards Ballater.'

That same year, the Queen, Prince Albert and the principal members of the Royal Court attended the Highland Gathering of the Braemar Society

(Colquhoun and Machell, 1927: p. 27). The Balmoral connection was reproduced in 1849 when the monarch and members of the royal family attended the Gathering at Braemar Castle on 6 September of that year. The Braemar Gathering by this time was becoming a traditional event in the social calendar of the new Highland landlords. Many of the nobility from Aberdeen, Perthshire and Forfarshire regularly presented themselves at these Highland Gatherings (Colquhoun and Machell 1927: p. 87). The Duke of Atholl and Sir Charles Forbes of Newe both brought Highlanders dressed in their respective clan tartans to the 1849 Braemar Highland Gathering. The *Scottish Diaries* of Queen Victoria (1868: 12 September 1850) provide a more detailed account of the Braemar Highland Gathering of 1850:

> We lunched early and then went at half past two o'clock with the children and all our party to the Gathering at the Castle of Braemar as we did last year. The Duffs, Farquharsons, the Leeds and those staying with them, and Captain Forbes and forty of his men who came over from Strath Don, were there ... There were the usual games of putting the stone, throwing the hammer and caber and racing up the hill at Craig Cheunnich ... Eighteen or nineteen started and it looked a very pretty sight to see them run off in their different coloured kilts.

A closer fusion between the Braemar Highland Gathering and Balmoral occurred in 1859 when the Braemar Highland Society was invited by the Monarch to hold a Highland Gathering at Balmoral on 22 September. What was by now becoming a tradition was reproduced in 1887, and again in 1890, 1898 and 1899 (Colquhoun and Machell, 1927). By this time, the Braemar Highland Society had become known as the Braemar Royal Highland Society. Symbolically, the bonding between Balmoral, the reigning monarch and the Braemar Gathering became enshrined in the position of the Highland chieftain. Such a tradition whereby the reigning monarch, or a member of the royal family, while on holiday at their summer residence at Balmoral, came to act as Highland chieftain to the Gathering at Braemar continues to the present day. This link between the past and the present is commented upon in the *Annual Book of the Braemar Gathering* (1980: p. 193):

> As laird of the Balmoral Estate Her Majesty has clearly demonstrated that she is vitally interested in the upkeep of the old traditions of the clans, the glens and their people and her presence each year at the Braemar Gathering is symbolic of this love of sport that has been a characteristic of her family right back to the days of her great-great grandmother Queen Victoria, who first graced the-Gathering with her presence in September 1848.

As indicated in the introduction, there can be no doubt about the influence of a particular social class in shaping the late-eighteenth and nineteenth-century Highland Gatherings. Certainly the Balmoralisation process produced and reproduced images of loyalty, royalty, tartanry and the clan figuration: cultural identity which Nairn (1988: p. 212) has recently referred to as the glamour of backwardness. In the *Scottish Diaries*, Queen Victoria (1868: 20 September 1868) constantly refers to herself as a clan chieftain, while Prince Albert not only manifested the tartan image by wearing the kilt but also designed and reproduced tartan kilts for the retainers of the royal party. The special value of the Highland Gathering was commented upon by the Duchess of Fife, the Princess Royal, when she said that at the Highland Gatherings, 'the laird and clansman, crofter and shepherd meet for the purpose of keeping alive the memories of the great past' (Colquhoun and Machell, 1927: p. 9). It is important not to forget that less than a hundred years earlier the same clan formation was viewed in an entirely different light. As a descendant of the Hanoverian monarchy, Queen Victoria symbolised the same forces of change that had led to the destruction of the Highland clan way of life. As such, the Balmoralisation process represents not so much a link with the traditions of the past, as a process of cultural transformation whereby traditions from the past, divorced from the social context in which they were originally situated and experienced, are in fact attributed with different meanings.

While historians, anthropologists and many others may have questioned Trevor-Roper's (1983) discussion concerning the invention of tradition, it is interesting to note that the essay by David Cannadine (1983) in the same collection of papers shows how much of what is regarded today as the British tradition was in fact hastily contrived towards the end of Queen Victoria's reign. Despite the continued centrality of the monarchy in British political, social and cultural life during this period, serious work by historians and sociologists on the subject of the monarchy is notable mainly by its absence. Indeed, as Nairn (1988) points out, serious curiosity about the British crown has been singularly lacking. Durkheim, of course, commented upon the integrative force of religious ceremony and ritual and the way in which such rituals embody, reflect, uphold and reinforce widely-held popular values. Marxists, by contrast, have argued that rituals and ceremonies have tended to be used by ruling élites as a means of consolidating their ideological hegemony over subordinate groups or classes. Yet it is important to stress not only that power relations within and between social fractions are a mediating factor in the selection of tradition, but also that traditions and rituals have to be understood within a developmental framework. When placed within the wider context of Highland history, various social class fractions, such as landlords, by virtue of their power, have been able to select, interpret and attribute different meanings to such cultural artefacts as tartanry, clans and what Nairn (1981) has referred to as the kitsch symbols of the Highlands.

Furthermore, it should not be forgotten that Queen Victoria was not only a Highland sporting landlady and patron to the Braemar Royal Highland Society Gathering but also, along with her husband, an active patron of the Society for Assisting Emigration from the Highlands and Islands of Scotland (Prebble, 1984: p. 202). The famine of the 1840s had served only to intensify the Highland landlord's hostility towards the crofting system. As Hunter (1976) indicates, by the late 1840s and early 1850s, most Highland landlords were well aware of the fact that a tenantry that could not produce an adequate rent would only lead to the bankruptcy of the landlord's estate. The landlords' evident conviction that emigration was the answer to the crofting problem stemmed both from the belief that sheep and deer provided a more reliable source of income, and from the conviction that emigration would once and for all rid the landlord of the dependent crofter. The actual machinery that was developed to enforce this ideology was provided for in the Emigration Advances Act of 1851 which, after being introduced into the House of Commons on 21 July, received royal assent from Queen Victoria on 7 August (Hunter, 1976: p. 77). The significance of the Act was not so much that it further facilitated clearances and enforced emigration, but that it set the seal of royal approval on the landlords' land policies.

With Queen Victoria as its patron, the Highlands and Islands Emigration Society functioned to assist the emigration of those crofters who wished to leave the Highlands. However, as I have already argued, there is a danger in placing too great a voluntaristic interpretation upon this process; if choice was significant, it reflected where the populace went and not the fact that they were forced to go. If a factor or landlord sets fire to your house and belongings, you have little choice but to move out. Quite simply, the traditional peasantry suffered as a result of the policies of the landlords. The Highlanders either remained to experience misery and struggle or moved reluctantly to other lands. For instance, the Society succeeded in sending some 5 000 Highlanders to Australia in the first five years of its existence (Hunter, 1976: p. 87). Of all the many thousands of people who left the Highlands during the 1840s and 1850s, few were as harshly treated as the Highlanders of Barra, South Uist and Benbecula. What they experienced can, in part, be gleaned from the recollections of Catherine MacPhee (Hunter, 1976: p. 81):

> Many a thing have I seen in my own day and generation, many a thing, O Mary Mother of the black sorrow! I have seen the townships swept, and the big holdings being made of them, the people being driven out of the countryside to the streets of Glasgow and to the wilds of Canada, such of them as did not die of hunger and plague and smallpox while going across the ocean. I have seen the women putting the children in the carts which were being sent from Benbecula and the Iachdar to Loch Boisdale, while their husbands lay bound in the pen and were weeping beside them, without power to give them a helping hand, though the women themselves were crying aloud and their little children wailing like to break their hearts. I have seen the big strong men, the champions of the coun-

tryside, the stalwarts of the world, being bound on Loch Boisdale quay and cast into the ship as would be done to a batch of horses or cattle in the boat, the bailiffs and the ground-officers and the constables and policemen gathered behind them in pursuit of them. The God of life and he only knows all the loathsome work of men on that day.

A Marxist interpretation of the clearances would be keen to highlight the degree of resistance, struggle and conflict between the landlords and crofters throughout the processes of clearance, emigration and the development of the sporting estates. Yet in the extensive literature concerning such processes during the 1850s and 1860s, no feature is more frequently commented upon than the crofters' lack of resistance to the evictions and the absence of violence, terrorism and intimidation. Such passiveness must not be exaggerated. In February and March of 1847, food riots erupted along the eastern and northern coasts of Caithness (Hunter, 1976: p. 90). During the 1850s, crofters denied access to land as a result of deer forest developments on Lewis marched into the forest and released the deer as a direct protest against the landlord (Jarvie, 1986b: p. 55). The flockmasters who looked after the sheep often resisted many deer forest developments since they threatened the flockmasters' existence by restricting the land available for sheep grazing (Jarvie, 1986b: p. 56). The Straithaird clearances of 1850 were resisted with some success by the crofters faced with eviction and subsequent emigration. But while there was a great deal of tension and conflict during the clearances, the conflict that emerged during the 1840s and 1850s consisted mainly of sporadic, relatively unconnected and isolated acts of defiance.

It is perhaps useful at this stage to highlight a number of important points that have been made in this chapter to date. It has been suggested: (i) that a number of factors, such as the declining fortunes of sheep farming and the inability of the crofters to obtain an income adequate for meeting their rent, meant that the Highland landlords of the Victorian period had to find alternative sources of income; (ii) that by the 1850s, the Highlands had already shown signs that they were to become a popular sporting playground for both the traditional aristocracy and the *nouveaux riches*; (iii) that the Balmoralisation process contributed to the popularity and identity of the Braemar Royal Highland Society and Gathering and gave the royal seal of approval to Highland sport in general; (iv) the same process contributed to the production and reproduction of images of loyalty, royalty, tartanry and clannishness so closely associated with Braemar; (v) the monarchy also associated itself with the machinery by which many Highlanders were forced to leave the Highlands; and (vi) that, in stark contrast to the leisure experiences of the sporting landlords, many people in the Highlands experienced life in terms of famine, poverty and congestion caused by overcrowding in the peripheral areas of the landlord's estate.

THE POPULARISATION PROCESS

The Balmoralisation process was not the only factor that led to the broader popularisation of the Highland Gatherings and Games. Improved communications and transport were certainly a significant factor too. The opening of the Deeside Railway from Aberdeen to Banchory in 1835, to Aboyne in 1859 and to Ballater in 1866 contributed to the popularisation of this Highland sporting form. Commenting on a general trend, McConnachie (1895: p. iii) estimated that Ballater alone was catering for 10 000 visitors a year by 1870 and that the coming of the railway had made Ballater the commercial capital of Upper Deeside. Braemar remained relatively isolated and yet fashionable for what McConnachie (1895: p. 108) refers to as a more select class of visitors. There is little doubt that the Balmoralisation process was inextricably linked to the process by which the Highland Gatherings and Games became popular during the latter half of the nineteenth century. When asked to comment upon the impact of Queen Victoria's attachment to the Highland Gatherings, a President of the Braemar Royal Highland Society replied (Braemar: Interview, 4 July 1986): 'There is no doubt, indeed, that the Games became popular because of the royal attachment ... When Queen Victoria came to the area a lot of landowners got the people who worked for them, stalkers, tenants, keepers, etc. ... rigged out in tartan ... Queen Victoria rigged out all her retainers in the Royal Stuart Tartan.'

The literary tradition of the kailyard also contributed in no small way to the popularisation process. The kailyard school originated in the last two decades of the nineteenth century and expressed a romantic nostalgia for a phase of Scottish life that had largely disappeared (Bold, 1983: p. 105). Like Scott's work of the early nineteenth century, the kailyard school contributed to a romantic, essentially Highland, image of the Scottish social formation. It contributed to what Nairn described as the cultural sub-nationalism which existed between about 1800 and 1920. As a form of nationalism, this cultural form was distorted. It was primarily created by a Scottish bourgeoisie who helped socially to construct a Scottish cultural identity that was unique and potentially a force of mobilisation against a British hegemony; at another level, it created a cultural illusion of Scotland which was essentially unionist and concealed many of the realities of Scottish and Highland exploitation (Carter, 1976 pp. 1-13).

The kailyard image of Scotland was underpinned by two main factors. Firstly, as mentioned above, the kailyard image, allied with the tartan – tourist image, helped to define a romantic cultural identity which was representative of unionist sentiments and feelings. Secondly, in countries such as America, Canada and Australia there developed an *émigré* market. A relative prosperity abroad allied with the distance from the realities of a lived way of life experienced by fractions of the Scottish social formation helped to create a market for kailyard writers who celebrated (mostly imaginary) Scottish images of the past. Such a form of cultural sub-nationalism abroad also helped to reinforce a nostalgic image of the Highlands in particular and Scotland in general.

Three central members of the kailyard school, Barrie, Crockett and Maclaren, presented an image of Scotland in which class relations were harmonious, as were the social relations which existed between the landlords and the crofters (Carter, 1976: p. 3). Scotland was portrayed as a country of bens and glens with the most prominent members of the Scottish social formation being ministers, doctors and housekeepers. Maclaren (1896) in particular was aware of the potential market to be expropriated from Balmorality and the growth of tourism particularly in the Scottish Highlands. As one writer commenting on the kailyard novels notes (Orwell, 1970: p. 409): 'Our picture of Scotland was made up of burns, braes, kilts, sporrans, claymores, bagpipes and the like, all somehow mixed up with the invigorating effects of porridge, protestantism and a cold climate. But underlying this was something quite different. The real reason for the cult of Scotland was that only very rich people could spend their summers there.'

The kailyard writers were not without their critics. Many commentators such as George Blake (1951) argued that the writers gratified a Victorian sentimentality and were victims of the chronic Scottish disease of nostalgia. Yet it was a romantic nostalgia, divorced from social reality, which helped to contribute to the popularisation process of the Highlands and Highland cultural forms. The Highland Gatherings and Games became popular in the light of this process. While it is not necessary to explain in

3.1: Highland Gatherings and Games, 1850-1910

Highland Gathering/Games	Year established
Pitlochry Highland Games	1852
Glenisla Highland Gathering	1852
Dunbeath Highland Games	1856
Alva Highland Games	1858
Ballater Highland Games	1864
Aboyne Highland Games	1867
Nairn Highland Games	1867
Argyllshire Highland Gathering	1871
Cowal Highland Gathering	1871
Airth Highland Games	1871
Luss Highland Gathering	1875
Abernethy Highland Games	1880
Halkirk Highland Games	1884
Brodick Highland Games	1884-6
Invercharron Highland Games	1888
Assynt Highland Games	1904

Source: Compiled from interviews, minute books, newspapers.

detail the development of every Highland Gathering and Games that emerged between about 1850 and 1920, it is important in the first instance to establish that such a process did occur.

Established in 1856, the Glenisla Highland Gathering is the annual Gathering of the Glenisla Highland and Friendly Society (Glenisla, Interview: 18 August 1986). The early minutes of the Glenisla Highland and Friendly Society (1895) state that the principal objectives of the Society are 'the preservation of Highland Garb and as far as possible the preservation of celtic customs and language'. Furthermore, the Glenisla minutes (1895) go on to express patriarchal, loyalistic and civilising concerns in that the Society and Gathering also purported to promote 'loyal, peacable, upright and manly conduct' while at the same time promoting 'social and friendly feelings amongst the inhabitants of the district'. Such traditional sporting events as hill-racing, putting the stone, tossing the caber and the playing of the piobaireachd were all major features of the inaugural Glenisla Highland Gathering. According to a Secretary of the Society, the first Glenisla Highland Gathering resulted from the inhabitants and crofters of the north and south end of the glens wanting to compete against each other in traditional Highland sports (Glenisla, Interview: 18 August 1986). A Gathering was accordingly organised by the Glenisla Highland and Friendly Society under the patronage of the Earl of Airlie, the major landowner in the glen at that time. His patronage also gave him a large measure of control over the proceedings. Not that the Earl of Airlie confined his sporting and land ownership interests solely to this glen. He also owned the sporting estate of Caenlochan which amounted to some 10 272 acres of Highland land (McConnachie, 1923: p. 55). It is interesting to note that the Secretary of the Glenisla Highland Gathering considered Lonach, Braemar, Aboyne and Glenisla to be the most authentic of all the Highland Gatherings and Games (Glenisla, Interview: 18 August 1986). The origins of the Lonach and Braemar Gatherings were considered in the last chapter; the Aboyne Highland Gathering and Games remain to be discussed.

While the *Aberdeen Free Press* and the *Buchan News* of 6 September 1867 make no mention of the Aboyne Games of 1867, they do mention the fact that Fife, Farquharson, Duff and Aboyne Highlanders were present at the Braemar Royal Highland Gathering of that year. However, the *Aberdeen Free Press* of 3 September comments upon the 'unalloyed success of the 3rd Annual Gathering and Games at Aboyne'. The paper goes on to comment that the Aboyne Games 'in fact, bids fair, with the exception that it has not yet been graced by the presence of royalty, to become the chief Gathering on Deeside'. Royal patronage was not long in coming, though, with the visit of the Prince and Princess of Wales in 1873.

According to a Secretary of the Aboyne Highland Gathering and Games, the first Highland Games there were fixed for 31 August 1867 (Aboyne, Interview: 2 April 1986). Events at these inaugural Aboyne

Games included light and heavy hammer throwing, putting the stone, caber tossing, Highland music and running and jumping. While the competitors had by 1870 to pay on entry, admission to the first Aboyne Highland Games was free. An annual ball was organised, with the price of tickets initially fixed at five shillings for ladies and gentlemen (Aboyne, Interview: 2 April 1986). The association with tartanry, clans, Highland chiefs and sporting landlords was produced and reproduced in the person of the Marquess of Huntly. As Highland chieftain to the Clan Gordon, the standard of the Marquess of Huntly was raised in the arena each year. To the Clan Gordon, the banners stood not only for a link with the past but also for a form of bonding; the flag symbolised both loyalty to the Highland chief and unity and solidarity within the clan itself (*Arbroath Herald:* September 1962). In much the same way, the raising of the national cross of St Andrew on the central flagstaff at the Aboyne Games was a symbolic form of bonding and loyalty to the monarchy at that time. It should not be forgotten that, by 1874, the Marquess of Huntly owned over 8 000 acres of land which included Huntly and Aboyne Castles, the hereditary seats of the Clan Gordon (McEwan, 1981: p. 33).

Like many Highland Gatherings and Games, the Aboyne Highland Gathering and Games produced and reproduced cultural images of tartanry, loyalty, royalty and clan life divorced from their original social context. The double role of sporting landlord and Highland Chief was in this instance dependent upon the patronage of the Marquess of Huntley.

Highland Games at Ballater also date back to the 1860s. By the time the railway had reached Deeside in 1886 Ballater had already emerged as a Highland retreat for what can be described, using Veblen's terms, as the 'leisure class' (McConnachie, 1895: p. 109). The Farquharsons of Invercauld were the major landowners that were associated with the Ballater Highland Games, although the Mackenzies of Glenmuick should also be mentioned. By 1874, the Invercauld estate stretched over 87 000 acres of Highland land (McEwan, 1981). As a past president of the Ballater Games commented, as feudal superiors in the parish of Ballater, the Farquharsons of Invercauld have historically performed the role of Highland chieftain to the Ballater Highland Games (Ballater, Interview: 7 August 1986). The following extracts taken from the minute book of the Ballater Athletic Club (1894: pp.1-2) provide some insights into the early beginnings of the Ballater Highland Games:

> At Ballater on the 16th July 1864 a meeting of the inhabitants of this parish was called by public notice. Mr Reid in the chair, it was prepared and unanimously agreed to that annual athletic games (open only to the parish) be established, and that Lieut. Col. Farquharson of Invercauld be president of the society.
>
> It was also agreed to hold the said games on Wednesday the 27th July, but at 12.00 noon on the church square, where the following

Games, be competed for; putting the stone, throwing the hammer, tossing the caber, dancing, running, vaulting, jumping, sack and barrow races ... A ball in connection with the Society to be held in the Mason's Hall at 9.00 pm.

As many of the subsequent programmes indicate, Ballater has attracted a great number of prominent athletes, dancers and pipers. In 1868, Donald Dinnie of Aboyne set new records in the heavy event. The famous Balmoral pipers also had a close connection with Ballater. Indeed, much of the Balmorality which structured the sporting practices at Braemar also influenced the sporting practices at Ballater. It is interesting to note that several of the rules and regulations which governed the nineteenth-century Ballater Highland games might be said to be indicative of a wider 'civilising process' whereby the Highlanders became less violent over a period of time. For instance, any member or person becoming quarrelsome or the 'worst for liquor' was immediately expelled from the Games Arena (Ballater, Programme 1985: p. 4). Any member deemed to be 'unreasonably disagreeing or insulting to the judge or the Committee' was, as a result of their behaviour, fined by those people in positions of power (Ballater, Programme 1985: p. 4)

Finally, as Webster (1973: p. 18) points out, a common rule applied to these early Gatherings and Games was the immediate disqualification of any competitor found to be wilfully tripping, knocking down or taking hold of any competitors, for example in the hill race. Such practices, so far as can be told, were all acceptable forms of behaviour during the eleventh-century hill race to the summit of Craeg Choinnich. In comparison with the early Gatherings and their antecedent forms, a degree of control was imposed upon the sporting practices of the Victorian period which resulted in less violent forms of behaviour.

Like many other Highland Gatherings and Games, the Argyllshire Gathering developed out of a milieu of social relations that were essentially patriarchal and controlled by the sporting landlord class. Founded in 1871, a past Secretary commented that the purpose of the inaugural, and subsequent, Argyllshire Gathering(s) was to provide a social event for the landowners of the County of Argyll (Argyllshire, Interview: 9 September 1986). In 1874, the major landowners included the Duke of Argyll and his kinsman the Earl of Breadalbane (McConnachie, 1923). Members of the Clan Campbell owned over 40 000 acres in Argyllshire (McConnachie, 1923: p. 50). Some of the sporting estates of that era included Benmore owned by the Duke of Argyll; Conaglen owned by the Earl of Morton; Blackorries and Glenlecknamuie owned by Lady Stratchcona; Jura, owned by Colin Campbell; Inversanda, owned by Major Maclean, and Glenforsa, owned by Col. Greenhill Gardyne (McConnachie, 1923: p. 57). All of these sporting landlords and many more would have been eligible to join the organising committee of the Argyllshire Gathering. The current Secretary commented that the minutes of the first meeting held on 25 August 1871 actually state that, in the first instance, membership of both the organising committee and of the Argyllshire Gathering itself would be restricted to 'landowners in the county and their sons' (Argyllshire, Interview: 9 September 1986). At the second annual general meeting of the Argyllshire Gathering held at Inveraray on the 30 April 1872, the following were decided (Malcolm, 1971: p. 5):

1. The object of the Gathering, which was the promotion of a   social meeting.

2. The qualification for membership which was restricted generally to landowners of Argyllshire, their sons and brothers, exceptional cases being referred to the Committee.

3. A committee to be appointed to manage the affairs of the Gathering.

4. A Ball to be held annually at such time and place as may be determined upon at the spring General Meeting.

The Argyllshire Gathering, probably more than any other Gathering, reproduces an extensive list of connections with the past in terms of clans, loyalist landowners, tartanry and Highland chieftains. Some of these associations during the Victorian period included the Campbells of Succoth, Airds and Arduaine; the Macleans of Duart, Ardghair and Lochbuie; the Stewarts of Appin and Achnacone; Macdougall of Macdougall; the Earl of Breadalbane and the Duke of Argyll, all of whom have displayed coats of arms at the Argyllshire Gathering (Argyllshire Programme, 1983: p 4). The forebears of many of these families fought on both sides in the Jacobite Rebellion of 1745. The particular influence of a sporting landlord class can be gleaned from the following (Argyllshire Programme, 1983: p. 3):

> The Argyllshire Gathering and Games grew out of a much earlier tradition for more warlike competition between the clans and you will be able to see the descendants of these clans both as spectators and competitors and even some of their chieftains within the members' enclosure. We are happy to say that our Gathering today is of an entirely peacable nature and spectators are unlikely to see any rivalry or feuds carried to violent remedies.

The discussion to date concerning the development of the Highland Gatherings and Games during the latter half of the nineteenth century has highlighted a number of important concerns which perhaps should briefly be summarised at this point. (i) It has been suggested that a popularisation process occurred between about 1850 and 1920 and that, while this was closely connected to Victorian 'Balmorality', this fact alone cannot be viewed as the sole causal factor; (ii) it has been demonstrated that there was in many cases an interlocking connection between the emerging sporting landlords of the Victorian period and positions of influence and power within the social composition of Highland Gatherings and Games; (iii) the traditions and practices associated with these Highland Gatherings and Games continued to be selective and divorced from their original social context; (iv) at one level the power of the landlord class to select, reproduce and transform many of the cultural meanings associated with this Highland sporting phenomenon may seem insignificant but at another level such changes were further indications of a continuing process of cultural dependency and marginalisation. The sporting landlords were the new cultural gatekeepers of Highland culture, a point which is essentially missing within the conventional wisdom on this topic; and (v) that the popularisation process of the Highland Gatherings and Games was inextricably linked to a broader popularisation process whereby the Highlands in general became a sporting playground for an amalgam of major and minor members of an emerging capitalist figuration. In drawing this chapter to a close it is necessary to return to the question of the ownership and control of land and the fluctuation of crofting experiences.

By the 1880s, Highland Gatherings and Games had been established at Cowal, Airth, Luss, Abernethy, Halkirk and Brodick, to name but a few. The early 1880s were also an important period in the development of sporting estates in that many foreign investors began to acquire property and land in the Highlands (Orr, 1982: p. 38). By 1855 the American, Bradley Martin, had acquired ownership of the Balmacaan estate, while by 1890 the Austrian Baron Schroder held the Attadale, Salriach and Ben Alder estates (Orr, 1982: p. 40). Blackmount Forest was sublet to the Austrian Ambassador, Count Karolyi for £2 000 in 1889 (Orr, 1982: p. 40). The American Winan brothers, having unsuccessfully attempted to persuade Sir James Mackenzie, the proprietor of Morvich and Inchroe, to evict the crofters from his land, eventually purchased no less that 200 000 acres of land between Kintail and Beaulx (Jarvie, 1986b: p. 51). William Louis Winan, on his own, held nine sporting estates in 1882, each estate being valued at around £10 845. By 1885 this land had increased to twelve estates with the property value of each rising to £11 855 (Orr, 1982: p. 32).

Foreign ownership of land did not, however, predominate within the sporting landlord class during this period. In 1863, the same year as Lord Dudley secured the lease of Dudley Forest, Lord Ashburton who already owned 15 000 acres in Hampshire, bought the Kinlockluichart estate and converted it into a deer forest for sporting purposes (McConnachie, 1923: p. 54). Lord Galway occupied Langwell Forest from 1863-75 (McConnachie, 1923: p. 55). The brewing industry was well represented through Sir Arthur Bass, Sir E. C. Guinness and S. Whitbread, all of whom had acquired substantial estates by 1885 (Jarvie, 1986b: p. 51). In 1869 Sir William Brooks leased the Glentanar estate from the Marquess of Huntly before purchasing it in 1890. By the 1900s, large tracts of land were still held by members of the British aristocracy such as the Duke of Westminster who owned the Reay estate; the Duke of Richmond and Gordon who owned the Glenfiddich, Glenavan and Glenmore estates, and the Duke of Atholl who owned Atholl lodge, together with the Dalnacaradock, Dalnamein, Dalnaspidal and Fealar estates. Finally, the Duke of Sutherland owned 1 180 000 acres of Highland land in 1920 which brought in an annual sum of £56 400 from sporting rent alone (Orr, 1982: p. 43).

But what of the crofters during the latter half of the nineteenth century? The popularisation process was not popular with all members of the Highland social formation, and the crofters in particular resisted the actions of the sporting landlords. If the 1850s and 1860s were times of relatively passive agitation by the crofters, the same cannot be said of the latter part of the nineteenth century. As was mentioned at the outset of this chapter, the passing of the Crofters Act of 1886 marked not only an important milestone in Highland social development, but also the end of a period of overt and intense tension, conflict and struggle between landlords and the crofters. While the Act did not solve all or even most of the problems facing the Highland social formation, it did guarantee the crofters security of land tenure. It also set up a Crofters Commission with the power to fix fair rents. It allowed tenants to bequeath their crofts to members of their families and it provided a degree of compensation to crofters who had previously relinquished their holding on the land (Napier Commission, 1884: S/R/O). The Crofters Act was not, however, freely given by a dominant class fraction of the time, but was secured in part by the actions of the crofters themselves (Hunter, 1976: p. 9). They were present in the making of their own history.

As the sporting landlords continued to develop their sporting estates and to push the crofters out to the edges of the Highlands, the crofters, flockmasters and many other less powerful class fractions developed numerous strategies to try and advance their struggle for land reform (Burnett, 1985: p.11). Scarcely a decade went by during the nineteenth century without various forms of popular protest against the actions of the landlords, whether they be Highland or sporting or both. In many cases, the forms of protest were similar in each instance:the destruction of sheep farms, the destruction of fences which surrounded deer forests, mass demonstrations against eviction orders, and the refusal to pay rent to the factors or landlords. The initial agitation which led to the security of tenure and fair rent provisions enshrined in the Crofters Act was the rent strike of 1882. The refusal of the Braes crofters on Skye to pay rent to Lord Macdonald until they had been returned their grazing rights culminated in a clash between crofters and police at Braes in April 1882 (McPherson, 1985). The actions of the Braes crofters acted as a catalyst for a series of rent strikes which, in totality, publicised widely the experiences of the High-land crofters during the latter part of the nineteenth century.

As an alternative to granting repressive assistance, the Gladstone government took other political steps to counter the growing unrest which, by 1886, had spread far beyond Skye to all corners of the crofters' counties (McPherson, 1985). The Queen's Speech promised a Bill to miti-gate the distressed conditions experienced by the Highlanders in general and the crofters in particular. Indeed, the pressure for legislation had be-come virtually irresistible following the report of the Napier Commission

in 1884. The evidence accumulated by the Commission during its tour of
the Highland and Islands constitutes one of the most revealing insights
into the conditions that were experienced by the crofters during the
nineteenth century. Elected spokespersons for each village poured out the
stories of how they had been dispossessed of land for sheep farms and
deer forests. The people of cleared villages had been forced either to
emigrate or to live on the edges of the Highlands, areas of land which
could not adequately support those who were dependent upon the actions
of the sporting landlords. The response of the Glenforsa crofters to the
Napier Commission's enquiries was typical of the many estates visited.
Meeting in the Temperance Hall in Salen, the Glenforsa crofters were
asked a series of questions (Napier Commission, 1884: Q46, pp. 200-1):

'How many of you present have enough land?' Not a hand was raised.

'How many are there who have not enough land?'
All hands went up.

'How many on the estate of Glenforsa have enough land to live on?'
'Two '

'How has it come about that there are so few holding land enough
and so many having so little?' 'The people have been cleared off
excellent and extensive land and sent hither and thither, some
settling in Salen, some in Tobermory, some in Glasgow and some in
foreign lands.'

The Napier Commission's report was sympathetic to the crofters'
cause, although its specific proposals for reform were, in the view of the
crofters, unacceptably modest. The crofters wanted legislation along the
lines of the 1881 Irish Land Act. As the government stalled, further unrest
developed. Rent strikes, attacks on sheriff's officers, and land raids by
crofters became increasingly commonplace. By May 1885, Gladstone introduced a Crofters Bill, but it fell with the government. By the New Year
a third liberal administration was in power, and the Crofters Act of 1886
was the one major piece of legislation to be successfully enacted by
Gladstone's short-lived government. Like practically every other piece of
reforming legislation, this Act resulted from a long period of struggle
during which time landlords tried to evict crofting community leaders.
The same leaders were frequently arrested and jailed, while crofters
themselves frequently battled with police in places such as Skye, Tiree,
Lewis and Sutherland.

Yet the 1886 Act is worth remembering for its shortcomings as well as
for its virtues. While the passing of its statutes was probably the most
important legislative event to shape the course of the Highland social
formation after the defeat at Culloden which symbolised the end of the
clan figuration, the Act fell well short of some of the crofters' demands for
the total liquidation of landlord power. Crucially, it failed to return the
land taken from the descendants of the crofters in preceding centuries.

Indeed, many would argue that the Act, in not restoring the lost lands to the dispossessed, did not resolve the Highland land question (Burnett, 1984: pp. 11-15). From the late 1880s right on into the 1920s there was a continuing but intermittent series of land raids. There were certain significant periods of activity, such as the immediate post-war outbreak of 1919-23. There were also certain key locations, notably Barra, the Uists, Lewis and Skye, but there were raids in other parts of the Highlands around the same time, notably in Argyll, Caithness and Perthshire (Burnett, 1984: p. 11) Although there were isolated incidents in the thirties and even in the post-Second World War years, raiding had effectively ceased by the early 1920s. The land question, while it remained an important issue after the 1920s, tended to be viewed within the wider context of Scottish political culture rather than a specific issue deserving attention in its own right. In particular, the land question contributed to the emergence of a distinctive socialist force whose location tended to be industrial Clydeside, as opposed to small-town Highland kailyards or isolated Highland bens and glens. The politicisation of Scottish culture after the 1920s drew heavily upon the memory of Highland rural struggles between the privilege, power and wealth of the landlords, and the poverty, eviction and powerlessness of the crofters. For instance, Tom Johnston and the Independent Labour Party used Scottish history, latent national consciousness, residual Irish and Scottish anti-landlordism and a general awareness of the complex interaction of various social groups in an attempt to produce some sort of counter-hegemonic bloc.

While the importance of the crofters' struggle should not be underestimated, its contribution to the discussion should not detract from the major focus of the analysis, namely the development of the Highland Gatherings and Games. The Victorian period marked a distinctive stage in the develop-ment of this Highland phenomenon. It was a stage which lasted from about 1840 until about 1920, during which time the Highland Gatherings and Games became respectable and popular sporting events. The Balmorali-sation process attracted a tremendous interest, particularly in the Braemar Royal Highland Gathering. The event has since become synonymous with loyalism, royalism and Balmorality. In the wake of this development, the Highlands became a sporting playground for the emergent sporting landlords. The popularisation processes referred to relates not only to the popularisation of the Highland Gatherings and Games, but also to the pro-cess by which sporting estates became a popular acquisition of many major and minor aristocrats during the nineteenth century. With specific reference to the Highland Gatherings, it is important to remember that the selection of traditions which contributed to this set of social practices helped to rewrite and redefine the traditions of the past. In stark contrast to the life of leisure associated with the sporting landlords during this period, large fractions of the Highland social formation continued to experience poverty, eviction from the land and possible forced emigration.

4

PROBLEMS OF MODERNITY

For these Highland Games are for the most part, merely fancy dress shows, got up for the entertainment of visitors who don't know the difference between a philabeg and a pibroch. These meetings, as at present constituted, do nothing to encourage the youth of the district in Highland Games, indeed they do not touch the life of the district any more intimately than does a travelling circus. For the games as at present constituted, are for the most part notoriously a draw for pot hunters and not even these are all Highlanders. When there is a reversion to the old form of Games, there will go, with much else, that which emulates the burlesque of the pantomime and music hall. (Donaldson, 1926: p. xxi.)

Writing about the development of the modern Scottish social formation is extremely difficult The modern period of development merges with what many writers refer to as contemporary society, and there is also a lack of sociological material and research referring specifically to the problems which emanate from the unique patterns of tension and struggle experienced by the social formation within which this study is located. Simon Pia (1987) has recently commented upon the surprising lack of serious discussion of Scottish sport, given its popular location within Scottish culture. With reference to the analysis of Scottish and Highland forms of sporting culture, there is rather little evidence on such important features as ownership and control, or any analysis of the complex way in which forms of sport are mediated by complex and specific forms of dependency and cultural domination.

Yet despite this complexity there can be no denying, I believe, that the dominant expression of today's Highland Gatherings and Games is characteristically modern. While the assumption should not be made that modernisation or indeed dependency proceeds in a unidirectional or straightforwardly progressive manner, one of the constant themes in what is an underdeveloped literature on the sociology of Scotland is that the dynamic relationships which are the very essence of this complex social formation are in fact mediated at both a national level and a Highland level by problems of dependency and cultural domination. Centralising forces which exist between a dominant metropole and a subordinate periphery result in the economic and cultural life of the periphery tending to become increasingly orientated towards the core, and consequently towards the values, tastes, and lifestyles of a dominant metropolitan elite. Any discussion on the modern Highland Gatherings and Games must be located within this changing nexus and pattern of social arrangements and tensions which developed after about 1920.

The first part of this chapter highlights the way in which the modern Highland Gatherings and Games have developed; the second part considers in a broader sense the problems of modernity experienced by fractions of the Scottish social formation; the third part refers to the notions of dominant and residual forms in drawing the strands of this analysis together.

THE MODERN HIGHLAND GATHERINGS AND GAMES

When sociologists, among others, have sought to examine the nature of modern sport and the way in which various social fractions experience it, they have directed their attention to an analysis of a number of factors and processes which have mediated and transformed sporting practices within industrial capitalist, primarily western, social formations (Hargreaves, 1986; Harvey and Cantelon, 1988; Holt, 1989). While some writers have limited themselves to forms of factor analysis, one of the strengths of both Gruneau's (1983) work and that of Dunning and Sheard (1979) is that these sociologists have located their discussion of sporting practices within the much broader context of social development. The past, as they quite rightly see it, is not insignificant to the present. While the Highland Gatherings and Games have developed as a result of a number of complex mediations between and within the patterns characteristic of the Scottish social formation, residual glimpses of the past still partially penetrate the modern expression of this set of cultural practices. Modern Highland Gatherings and Games, while they have developed in a number of multifaceted ways from their folk origins, are still, in part, constituted from those earlier social practices and traditions.

Before highlighting some of these many developments, I should like to consider at a more concrete level some of the many individual Highland Gatherings and Games. What follows is not a complete discussion of all the modern Highland Gatherings and Games; the social practices and sporting traditions at Cowal, Airth, Argyllshire, Halkirk and Braemar provide a representative cross-section of present-day traditions.

In 1910, 51 000 spectators attended the Cowal Highland Gathering with prize money amounting to over £160. Professional wrestlers were given £10 if the weather was wet and £20 if it was fine (Cowal committee Papers: p. 4). The committee agreed that the rule relating to the compulsory wearing of the kilt should be enforced. Between 1914 and 1918 the events were abandoned. They were resumed after the First World War and after 1932, the total prize money exceeded over £2 000 (Oban Times: 2 July 1932). By the autumn of 1938 the tartan tradition was symbolised further with tartan flags of various clans decorating the main street of Dunoon. Like many other Highland Gatherings and Games, many local rules were rationalised after the Second World War with the advent of the Scottish Games Association which was formed in 1946 (Scottish Games Association Handbook, 1986). While many of the Victorian landlords had died by the end of the Second World War, a residual fraction of this social class continued to patronise the Cowal Gathering, including titled landowners such as the Duke of Argyll, Sir Ivar Colquhoun of Luss and Lord Maclean of Duart who had been regular senior stewards since the 1930s (Cowal Programme: 1984). To this day the march of a thousand pipers is one of the Highland events which continues to be associated with Cowal.

Held on the last Friday and Saturday of August, the Cowal Highland Gathering and Games continued through to the present day to be the home of the world adult and junior Highland dance competitions. In 1985 over 300 men and women dancers from Dunoon, Helensburgh, Canada, Australia, America and many other nations where Scottish émigrés had gone, competed for the Cowal Gold Medals and for cash prizes ranging from £25 for first to £7 for fourth position (Cowal Programme, 1985: p. 10). Over ninety-four events continued to come under the auspices and control of various officials from the Scottish Amateur Athletic Association, the Scottish Pipe Band Association and the Scottish Games Association. A fusion of traditional and modern sporting practices includes piping, dancing, throwing events, cycling, handicap events and metric running races from 100 metres to 5 000 metres (Cowal Programme, 1985: p. 10). Commenting on the history of the Cowal Gathering, a committee member stated 'that while popularity probably reached its heights during the 1930s, the Gathering can still pay out over £3 000 in cash prizes and draw a sizeable crowd depending on the weather' (Cowal, Interview: 11 June 1986).

Like those of Cowal, the Airth Highland Games were founded in 1871. During the first decade of the twentieth century the wife and daughter of the Earl of Dunmore presented prizes for the best dressed Highlander in attendance (Airth Papers, unpublished). Although no games were held during the First World War, 1 500 people attended the Airth Games of 1918, and by 1922 bookmakers were setting up betting stalls alongside popular working-class Lowland sports like whippet racing and pony trotting (Airth Programme, 1922: p. 7). Traditional Highland sporting practices such as dancing and heavy events still formed the core of the programme. By the 1930s, the Airth Games had become part of a week-long local Highland Games circuit in which contests were held at Bannockburn on the Monday, at Airth on the Tuesday, at Torreyburn on the Wednesday, at Culross on the Thursday and at Kirkaldy on the Friday

(Airth, Interview: 12 April 1986). During the 'golden years' of the 1920s and 1930s, record crowds of over 10 000 regularly watched competitors compete for prize money of up to £200 in some events (Airth, Interview: 12 April 1986). Like the Cowal Games, after 1946 the Airth Games continued to be rationalised and recorded by incipient bureaucracies such as the Scottish Games Association.

After the Second World War, the Airth Games, like many other games, had to compete with many other popular developments such as wireless parties. *The Falkirk Herald* of 10 July 1961 underlined the commercial mass media development as being one of the modern problems which intruded into all aspects of local people's lives. During the 1950s and 1960s the Airth Highland Games survived, although attendances and finances dropped for a number of complex reasons. By the 1980s, however, largely due to the efforts of local people and a certain degree of sponsorship from an amalgam of major and minor *petit bourgeois* organisations, the Airth Highland Games had come to be able to offer prize money in excess of £2 550 (Airth Papers, unpublished). The programmes and marketing brochures of the modern Airth Highland Games, illustrating tartan-kilted men tossing the caber, point out that the heavy events at Airth contribute to qualification for the Tamnavulin Glenlivet Scotch Whisky Trophy (Airth Programme, 1985). Tartan dancers from overseas continue to compete. One member of the Committee enthusiastically remarked 'that the tourists come along to see the swing of the kilt, and the tossing of the caber' (Airth, Interview: 12 March 1986). 'Come to Airth', another re-marked, 'and you will see a full programme of events, something going on all the time, never a break in the programme' (Airth, Interview: 12 April 1986).

Like Cowal and Airth, the Argyllshire Gathering was also formed in 1871. During the early years of the twentieth century, gate-money was raised at the level of 1s 3d for children and 3s for adults (Oban Times: 20 August 1930). The Gathering, particularly up to the Second World War, continued to attract large numbers of the landed gentry who spent their summer season in the Highlands. The *Oban Times* from the 1930s onwards continued to print large lists of those who attended the Gathering which was held over two days in September. For instance, the Argyllshire Gathering of 1938 was attended by the Duke and Duchess of Montrose, Sir Charles Maclean of Duart, Lady Margaret MaCrae, Sir Colin MaCrea, and Maclachlan of Maclachlan, to name but a few (*Oban Times:* 17 September 1938). Traditional events, as now, predominated in the programme of the Argyllshire Gathering, with the playing of the piobaireachd being of a notably high standard. Compared to the £50 prize money awarded as first prize in the open piobaireachd event in 1985, £3 was awarded in 1932 (*Oban Times:* 16 July 1932). Like other Highland Gatherings and Games, the Argyllshire was suspended during the two world wars and came under the auspices of various incipient bureaucracies after about 1945.

Admission rates during the 1980s have been increased to 60p for children under fourteen and £1.80 for adults. Prize money which amounts to over £3 000 is acquired through sponsorship from a number of local entrepreneurs such as Half Way House Enterprises and Economic Forestry Limited (Argyllshire Programme, 1983). Like Airth, the heavy events at the Argyllshire Gathering contribute to the Tamnavulin Glenlivet Scottish Whisky circuit. Most of the Games records in heavy events are currently held by the English former Olympic gold medalist in the shot-put, Geoff Capes, who like other competitors has to compete in the kilt (Argyllshire Programme, 1983: p. 4). The present chieftain to the Argyllshire Gathering is the current Duke of Argyll and, as the current secretary pointed out, 'The Argyllshire Gathering Ball continues to be one of the top Balls in the country, just a social gathering for the members and their parties, regularly attended by nobility and royalty' (Argyllshire Interview: 9 July 1986). Indeed, while Gatherings in general may have changed in a number of ways, the Argyllshire Gathering continues to be a social club consisting of the landed proprietors of Argyll and their sons and daughters (Argyllshire Interview: 9 July 1986). It is interesting to note at this point that some sixty-seven individuals or companies between them own 47 per cent of the land in Argyllshire (McEwan, 1975: p. 201).

The Halkirk Highland Games, stated the Halkirk Secretary, date back to at least 1884 (Halkirk, Interview: 4 August 1986). The modern Halkirk Highland Games have experienced various phases of decline and renewal. While crowds of around 1000 were considered large in the early 1920s, these have gradually increased to around 6000 during the 1980s (Minutes, Halkirk: 1984). Chieftain of the Halkirk Highland Games during the first part of the twentieth century was traditionally Viscount Thurso of Ulbster, with the present Lord Thurso, owner of Thurso Castle, continuing to be chieftain to the games during the 1980s (Caithness Courier: 3 August 1983). The Halkirk Highland Games did not take place during the 1914-18 War nor during the period 1939-52. A minute of 6 May 1925 noted that the balance in hand after the games was £13 7s. In 1927 the secretary was asked to obtain 1 000 tickets at 1s 3d and 350 tickets at 3d. By 1928, novelty events had included a ladies' football match, a baby show, and clay pigeon shooting events (John O'Groats Journal: 26 August 1938). However, traditional Highland events such as piping, dancing, heavy events and foot races continued to be the main attractions. During the 1950s traditional events continued to be judged by an army of stewards and judges from various associations, gate-money remaining steady at around £3 000.

One of the major changes, commented a past committee member, is that the 'crowds have got bigger as the better professional athletes have come to Halkirk' (Halkirk, Interview: 4 August 1986). Transport was difficult during the early days, but, today a competitor can take away as much as £200 in prize money from the Halkirk games and then move on to another Highland Games. 'The cash prizes have had to increase', adds the secretary, 'if we wanted to attract the best athletes such as Capes' (Halkirk, Interview: 4 August 1986). While prize money was at the £100 level during the 1920s, the cash money on offer in 1976 was £1 700 and in 1986, £3 000 (Halkirk, Interview: 4 August 1986). First prize in the open piobaireachd carried a cash award of £50. Residual glimpses of the agrarian folk origins of the Highland Gatherings can also be found at Halkirk in such events as tossing the shief, a tightly bound bail of hay. The Clan Gunn are closely associated with the Halkirk Highland Games just as the Wallace, Forbes and Duff clans are closely associated with the Lonach Highland Gathering and Games (Lonach, Interview: 20 August 1986). It is also interesting to note that, in the view of one of the organising members, the Highland Games of the Lowlands tend to be different from those in the Highlands. 'More piping, more dancing, more heavies, and no bookies or betting give the Highland Games of the Highlands a more Highland flavour' (Halkirk, Interview: 4 August 1986).

The Gathering of the Braemar Royal Highland Society has also developed in a number of ways, although the dominant images of Balmorality, loyalty and royalty still remain. The Queen remains the chieftain to the Braemar Gathering, although close associations also remain between Braemar and the Duke and Duchess of Fife, Captain Farquharson of Invercauld and Captain Alexander Ramsay of Mar (Braemar Programme, 1986). Tartan programmes can be bought at the price of 25p, while the entrance charge during the 1980s stands at £1.50p. Sponsorship from an amalgam of major and minor consortiums such as British Petroleum, Grant's Scotch Whisky, the Glenfiddich Pure Malt Whisky Group and the Taylor Woodrow Group enables Braemar to offer cash prizes of between £75 and £5 in over sixty-two events (Braemar Programme, 1983). Rule Four states that all competitors must be dressed in Highland Costume, except for running and jumping competitions in which competitors must wear University running dress, a comment which perhaps reflects the social class associations which continue to mediate the Games (Braemar Programme, 1983).

Seen in isolation, the differences between the many different Highland Gatherings and Games of today may be viewed by many as being insignificant. Yet viewed in the context of long-term development, it is possible to distinguish between earlier forms of Highland sporting practices and those which are characteristically modern (Elias, 1978a: p. 12). Few people would argue with the fact that the modern Highland Gatherings and Games have developed in a number of multifaceted ways. Increasing rates of commodification, professionalisation, incipient bureaucratisation and rationalisation are but a few of these developments. As a particular form of culture, Highland Gatherings produce and reproduce romantic cultural images of social patterns and arrangements that are no longer dominant within the social formation. Many, if not all, have been affected by the equalising process referred to by Elias as functional democratisation, yet residual groups of powerful landlords and descendants of the Victorian bourgeoisie still contribute to The modern Highland Gathering.

I want to refer to four phenomena indicated in these descriptions before moving on to a broader discussion of the problems of modernity experienced by the Scottish social formation. Firstly, in contrast with the original Highland Gatherings, in which there were no codified rules, no standard format and no apparatus for recording times, records and contests, the present Highland Gatherings and Games have become considerably more formal. Elaborate written rules are worked out pragmatically and legitimated by rational bureaucratic means (Dunning and Sheard, 1979: p. 33). It is less than a hundred years since the Highland Gatherings and Games began to be regulated by judges, stewards, written rules and records in relatively standardised and rationalised forms. The dominant interpretation of the modern Highland Gatherings is no longer one of casual, spontaneous and loosely-organised contests, but rather one of rationalisation and bureaucratisation. Control has increasingly been exercised through the medium of a bureaucratic chain involving members of the Scottish Games Association, the Scottish Amateur Athletic Association, the Scottish Pipe Band Association and local community organising committees, to name but a few of the multi-polar points of control. Such developments are indicative of a characteristically modern trend towards rationalisation and bureaucratisation.

Secondly, the Highland Gatherings have become increasingly subject to processes of commodification and professionalisation. It is important to distinguish between the different facets of these processes. Some Highland Gatherings are organised on a profit-maximising basis in which investment is orientated towards the accumulation of capital. A great number of Highland Gatherings and Games, though, whilst highly commercialised, do not operate on this basis. The objective is rather to break even or operate at a low cost in order to maintain financial viability, though these sporting practices can stimulate the accumulation of capital indirectly by providing a market for goods and services such as whisky, tartan rugs, tourism services and catering services. As with sport in general, capital accumulation also results from sponsorship and advertising such as that involved in the association between Tamnavulin, Glenlivet Scotch Whisky and Chevron Petroleum UK Limited, although individuals and companies may invest in sport for non-economic purposes, such as that of gaining prestige from being associated with a popular cultural activity, prestige which may or may not ultimately enhance the image of the investor (Hargreaves, 1986: pp. 114-37). All of these complex developments have contributed to the dominant interpretation of today's Highland Gatherings and Games as being one of increased commodification and professionalisation.

Thirdly, there is the issue of cultural domination which is accomplished in part when home-grown cultural forms such as traditional regional music, dance and games are seen by local people to be less attractive and less meaningful than the tastes, sports and pastimes of the economic and cultural capitals of the metropolis (Whitson, 1983). Modern Highland Gatherings and Games continually have to struggle for popularity with numerous cultural products and alternative sporting forms such as football, rugby, cricket, snooker, and American football, all of which are disseminated through the communications network of radio, cinema and television. It is not out of context here to refer to the problems facing modern shinty as discussed by Innes (1978: p. 11), who argues that every effort is required 'to keep the game alive in the face of the glamour which television coverage confers on the sports of the South'. The wearing of the football shirts of Rangers, Celtic, Manchester United, Liverpool and Argentina indicate the challenges and inroads that are made by a more dominant metropolitan culture. These examples and many more raise the questions of dependency and cultural domination that are experienced by Highland Gatherings and Games as a result of modernising and centralising forces.

Finally, there is the issue of social class and the continuing association, albeit residual, with the sporting landlords. As Gruneau (1979: p. 2) indicates, a failure of much of the writing on sport and social class is the lack of an adequate distinction between levels of athletic participation and levels of organisational leadership. In the first instance it is important to highlight the fact that the term 'democratisation' as it is used in this study should not be taken as implying that equality has been achieved. It refers to a process of growing equalisation over time, and is consistent with the continued existences of degrees of every-significant inequality. As indicated earlier, the fact that the Highland Gatherings now have a great participation rate in terms of gender, social class and racial fractions does not by any stretch of the imagination mean that the resources that the people involved have at their disposal are equal. It is also necessary not to overstate the degree of democratisation that has occurred at the level of organisation control. But a social transformation has occurred, and the power differentials between groups, still vast within industrial capitalist social formations, when placed within the context of long-term social-development can be said to have diminished relatively. Landlords such as those mentioned already, plus others like Sir William Gladstone of Frasque and Glendyer, or Viscount Cowdray, still exert a cultural and structural influence upon the modern Highland Gatherings. Yet when viewed against nineteenth-century social practices, it is clear that a degree of democratisation has developed in that community control is greater today than it was in the nineteenth century. This should not be taken to imply that the question of landlord control over the land in the Highlands is no longer a problem today but simply that, at the level of organisational control, the modern Highland Gatherings have experienced a *relative degree* of democratisation.

PROBLEMS OF MODERNITY

The developments mentioned so far have not taken place outside the context of developments experienced by the Scottish social formation as a whole. While different regional fractions may have developed at different rates, the general social relationship between the British state and the Scottish social formation has become increasingly problematic, a development which has been expressed, in part, in terms of nationalist and socialist aspirations by national and social class fractions. Late-twentieth-century Scots should be grateful that the democratic socialist view that human needs and the common good are the principal objectives which a political system must serve are not the sole prerogatives of any one party, but are aspirations which are widely shared in Scottish life. Industrial decline and renewal both in modern Scotland as a whole and in the Highlands in particular have prompted the British state to become more closely embroiled within the social fabric of the Scottish way of life. The growing influence of a dominant metropolitan élite and the degree to which such a dominant class fraction has the power to regulate and control traditional ways of life is certainly one of the problems of modernity facing the Highland social formation. While the relational patterns which characterise the present social fabric of Scotland have themselves developed in a number of ways, it is precisely the forces of relative domination and dependency and a concern over cultural identity which have, in part, shaped many of the social struggles and tensions within what James Kellas (1968) has referred to as a 'Modern Scotland' which emerged after about 1920. What has prompted a renewed debate about the relationship between Scottish culture, socialism and nationalism has undoubtedly been the Thatcher experience. The 1987 general election results in Scotland which left the Conservatives with only ten of the available seventy-two seats was not so much a pro-Nationalist statement as an anti-Conservative or in particular an anti-Thatcherite bloc vote. It is against this changing nexus and pattern of social arrangements and tensions that a discussion on the development of the modern Highland Gatherings and Games must be located.

While congestion, poverty and land hunger may have been some of the common experiences of the Highland way of life during the nineteenth century, depopulation and a relatively low standard of living have been recognised as but two of the key developments which have affected the social structure of the Highlands during the twentieth century (Hunter, 1975; Dickson, 1982). Sporadic oil-related developments during the 1970s may have brought a short-term respite for some, but as far as control of resources by local people is concerned, decisions have tended to be external to the local communities affected by these developments, if not external to the British state apparatus itself. Oil-related developments certainly contributed, in some areas, to changing expectations, aspirations and improved rates of communication, factors which were all experienced at various rates by those Highland communities affected by oil. These and many other developments, such as expanding educational opportunities, have contributed to bringing both the Highlander and the Lowlander, at different rates, more completely into the mainstream of British, social, economic and cultural life.

What is particularly significant about modern Scotland as a whole is the fact that, while fractions of the Highland social formation had experienced problems of dependency in the past, such problems had not been experienced by the Scottish social formation as a whole. The dominant causal factor affecting the development of the Scottish social formation after about 1920 was the changing patterns of cultural domination and dependency brought about by the centralising forces that existed between an English metropole and a Scottish hinterland (Nairn, 1981; Dickson, 1982). The activities of the British state apparatus and a southern metropolitan class have continued to mediate the social fabric of the Highlands. Problems of modernity were simultaneously experienced differently and yet similarly by the Highlands and the rest of the Scottish social formation. A total social transformation involving increasing rates of dependency developed after about 1920.

It is important at this point to mention the analysis put forward by Nairn (1981). Briefly, Nairn's thesis is that, up until about the 1920s, Scotland never developed a national political culture. Having never been faced with the dilemma of dependency and underdevelopment, until this period the Scottish middle classes were not compelled to mobilise the Scottish people in a developmental struggle. In the absence of any nationalist political culture, what evolved instead was a romantic cultural sub-nationalism which had to be romantic in that it could not be political in an oppositional sense (Nairn, 1981: p. 156). This cultural sub-nationalism consisted of three prominent strands: the view of the *émigré*, kailyardism, and tartanry. For Nairn, the logic of nationalism was that it was closely connected with the unevenness of capitalist development and the relationship that arose between two cultures at different stages of economic advancement. According to Nairn, it was a distinctly modern Scottish problem.

A sociological examination of nationalism would require a thorough historical exposition of nationalist movements in Scottish history. The development of Scottish nationalism, however, is not the central focus of analysis here. The idea that global processes of centralisation might engender a reaction and that nation-states could become the vehicle for expressing opposition to such trends is relatively unexplored (Mears, 1986: p. 310). Indeed, Mears suggests that it might be more accurate to think of waves of centralisation that in turn trigger off centrifugal forces. National unification and mobilisation of national sentiments have often been viewed as a prerequisite for stable political development which in itself is often seen as a precondition for modernisation and economic development. Furthermore, the development of nationalism in the Scottish sense is not the same as saying that a politicisation of Scottish culture emerged after about 1920. Nationalist forces certainly played a part in this, but so did a number of other political developments.

While flaws may be found in Nairn's approach to culture, there are several useful contributions that his thesis makes to the discussion at hand. Firstly, it highlights the fact that the period after about 1920 was marked by an increasing rate of politicisation of Scottish culture which resulted, in part, from a reaction against increased British state intervention in Scottish affairs. Such interventions did not go uncontested by a number of social fractions. Secondly, Nairn's theory of romantic cultural sub-nationalism relates to a problem of modernity in that romanticism amongst various class fractions continues to mediate the reality of dependency and slower rates of development experienced by fractions of the Scottish social formation. Thirdly, it highlights the fact that nationalism and socialism need not be poles apart ideologically. Yet while accepting the logic of Nairn's work there are still certain inadequacies concerning the notion of culture that is used. Not only does his aesthetic, literate, humanistic approach to culture dismiss the possibilities of any oppositional currents of resistance that might emerge through popular culture, but more importantly it fails to highlight the complexity of interpenetrating relationships that occur between various social fractions at different levels.

It is, however, appropriate to apply Nairn's concept of cultural subnationalism to an analysis of the modern Highland Gatherings, both at the level of theory and that of concrete data. Firstly, there is the image of Scotland as expressed through the eyes of the *émigré* The Highland Gatherings, golf at St Andrews, tartan armies, whether it be Ally's or Jock's, and Hampden Park all contribute to a broad strand of cultural identity which also includes the view of Scotland as a country of small crofts, bens, glens and stags at rest on mist-enshrouded slopes – not to forget granny's 'Highland Home' which always tends to gain appeal and credibility with distance. Many of these images are portrayed in the Highland Games programmes and lived out in practice by the *émigré* at the level of spectator participation. The important point to remember is that it is the emotional and romantic significance bestowed on these and many other symbols which has not only given rise to a distortion of history but have also guaranteed a world market for all of what Nairn refers to as the 'standard kitsch symbols of Scottish cultural identity'. As Chapman (1978) has indicated, Scottish culture has drawn heavily on a Gaelic vision of cultural identity.

Secondly, there is the legacy of the kailyard strain, not only in literature but also in television and film. The origins of this romantic literature have already been briefly mentioned in this text. It is a body of literature in which harmonious class relations are portrayed and no conflict of material interest ever mediates the social relations which exist between landlord and crofter or clan chief and clansfolk. Kailyard fiction tends to portray Scottish life as seen through the windows of the Free Kirk manse which stood for Presbyterian fundamentalism and a rejection of state interference in church matters (Jarvie, 1986). The kailyard strain eventually gave rise to the modern cultural definition of Scotland as consisting wholly of small towns, churches, and harmonious class relations. The central figure within this social formation were ministers, school teachers, doctors, housekeepers, and a continual supply of clansfolk and Highland chiefs. Modern examples include media presentations of *Dr Finlay's Casebook*, *Rob Roy Macgregor* and many more. While *Chariots of Fire* and *Local Hero* provided a boost to the Scottish film industry, the images of Scotland they portrayed were again selective of strains typical of the kailyard literature.

The third factor which, in a multitude of different forms, continues not only to define a Scottish cultural identity but also Scottish sporting identity, is tartanry. Both the view of the *émigré* and modern kailyardism have relied heavily upon tartanry as the dominant expression of Scottish culture. Tartan football armies and Highland Gatherings and Games immediately spring to mind. Highland Games programmes and marketing brochures, both at the level of local games and the level of the Scottish Tourist Board, are heavily dependent upon tartan imagery. Another example would be the tradition found at the Cowal Highland Gathering of lining the main street of Dunoon with tartan banners including those of the Mackintosh, Gunn, Macduff and Stewart clans (Cowal Programme, 1984). 'With the hills in the background and the sounds and sights of the pipe bands, it is a moving sight for tourists and regulars alike', commented one of the organisers (Cowal Interview: 11 June 1986). Such romantic symbols, upon which Scotland has become culturally and to a degree economically dependent, are quite divorced from historically lived experience. It is doubtful if the Highlanders of the pre-1745 epoch envisaged their ultimate inheritance as being that of pictures on whisky bottles, shortbread tins, Highland Games programmes, Scottish tourist brochures or even plaited socks. As an aspect of Scottish culture in general, and of Highland culture in particular, tartanry in its original context was virtually destroyed towards the end of the eighteenth century. Furthermore, at the level of modern popular culture it should be mentioned that, not even on Highland Games day do you see the bulk of the Highland people walking around in kilts, scarfs or other tartan fabrics.

As Elias (1983: p. 222) points out, romanticising impulses can usually be located amongst particular elevated classes whose own claims to power are essentially unfulfilled despite their social rank. This type of compulsion may have characterised the romantics of the Victorian bourgeoisie during the nineteenth century, but the process of romanticisation may also be at work in industrial urban populations. An industrialisation process, experienced in terms of constraint and rationalisation, often led to a situation in which rural workers who migrated to the metropolis were idealised by industrial working class fractions as symbols of a better past or of a relatively free and natural life (Elias, 1983: p. 214). These statements should not be taken out of context in the sense that, what Elias specifically refers to in his discussion on this point is the contrasting constraints between rural and industrial environments.

While Scottish culture continued to be dependent upon a romantic cultural sub-nationalism after 1920, it would be misleading and incorrect to argue that a political culture did not evolve in reaction to forces of relative dependency and cultural domination. While Scottish culture experienced a higher degree of politicisation after about 1920, a number of interrelated factors, and not just nationalist concerns, gave rise to what Young (1979) refers to as the rousing of the Scottish working class. It is not necessary to provide a lengthy discussion on the politicisation of Scottish culture to illustrate that such a development did in fact take place. A great deal of flux, tension and struggle did emerge after 1920 and yet the relative failure, particularly of the radical working class movements, might also be explained in part by the relative centralising forces of dependency and cultural domination.

Immediately after the 1914-18 war, Scots formed numerous political, cultural and trade union groups to try and advance their struggle for class and national emancipation. Scarcely a decade went by without continuing tensions and strains ebbing and flowing. For instance: (i) by 1900 the Crofters' Party of 1886 had been reabsorbed into the Liberal Party, yet land raids continued into the 1920s. While the popular challenge to landlord power was effectively reduced after about 1920, sporadic land raids by crofters took place in the 1930s and 1940s; (ii) a key feature of the inter-war years was the emergence of Labourism in Scotland under the leadership of such people as John McLean, John Wheatly, and Ramsay Macdonald. The inter-war years were characterised in Glasgow by work stoppages, rent strikes and massive labour unrest against the conditions experienced in post-1918 modern industrial Scotland; (iii) the development of Scottish renaissance literature and in particular the writings of MacDiarmid, Edwin Muirhead and Neil Gunn, all gave strength to the Scottish nationalist politics which developed after 1920 and which possibly reached a height of activity during the period leading up to the 1979 referendum on devolution. A nationalist movement, although having various degrees of success, has never had a strong basis of electoral support in Scotland; and (iv) while the popular myth about Red Clydesdale was that the socialist revolution was imminent, the chances of it occurring were probably small because, despite the emergence of a number of charismatic leaders such as John Wheatley, David Kirkwood, William Gallacher, James Maxton and many others, the only leader with any theoretical notion of how a revolution might be constructed was John Maclean (Smout. 1986: p. 272).

More fundamentally, the relationship between the Scottish social formation and the British State apparatus changed during this period of crisis.

While Scotland had been a nominally equal partner within the Act of Union between 1707 and 1920, after this period the Scottish relationship with the British state apparatus was one of a client or dependent formation (Dickson and Clarke, 1982). However, the crisis on Clydesdale was a very real crisis for the British state. As Smout (1986: p. 268) recounts, the 'citizens of Glasgow woke on January 20th 1919 to find six tanks in the cattle market, a howitzer at the city chambers and machine-gun nests at the hotels and the post-office'. Even the most liberal of social historians has agreed that the Scottish working class has always been further to the left of the political spectrum than their English equivalent (Lenman, 1977). Why, then, given the high degree of politicisation, did the popular movements of the 1920s fail in their challenge against the British state? The two most common answers given to this question are, firstly, that the events of the 1920s have been mythologised and romanticised, and that a socialist revolution was not what the working class was struggling for (Smout, 1986: p. 268). This may or may not have been the case. Analysis should leave open the possibility that the romantic factor was real, but the evidence does indeed suggest that post-war Scottish working class movements were further to the left in the political spectrum than their English counterparts.

The second explanation given is illustrative of the problems of dependency and cultural domination experienced by the wider Scottish social formation after this period. It has been suggested that, in response to the radical challenges of the post-war years, the leaders of the Scottish working class were effectively absorbed and constrained by English-based trade unionism and British parliamentary action (Dickson and Clarke, 1982). Of the Clydesdale Labour MPs elected to Westminster immediately after the war, only Maxton returned to the ILP. The majority of Labour socialists appear to have become part of a Parliamentary environment that was totally out of sympathy with their ideology and, as Smout (1986: p. 272) argues, they allowed themselves to be absorbed into the more metropolitan and less radical environment of London society. Furthermore, while Scotland up until 1920 existed as an equal partner within British industrial capitalism, dependency after this period resulted in part from the tendency to relocate capital south of the border. Control on an increasing number of levels was located outside of Scotland. This point has been emphasised recently by the 1980s *Report* of the General Assembly's Church and nation Committee (Church and Nation Committee *Report*, 1985: N/L/S.

In addition to these two explanations, it could be suggested that British state intervention in the Highlands is an example of how centralising forces can give rise to problems of modernity, dependency and cultural domination. State policies in the Highlands have had various rates of success and failure but many of the problems of modernity experienced by the Highland social formation have been exacerbated by the fact that whole communities and ways of life were, and continue to be, dependent upon decisions taken by groups or social class fractions far removed from the majority of people who live out their lives on the periphery. Some examples of this state intervention in the Highlands during the twentieth century may serve to draw attention to some of the specific problems of modernity and dependency experienced by the Highland social formation.

By 1912, the Congested District Boards and the Crofters Commission had come under the control of the Department of Agriculture. The Hilleary Committee of 1930 suggested that the government should invest more money in the Highlands (Adams, 1976: p. 425). The Taylor Commission of 1951 contributed to the re-establishment of the Crofters Commission but concluded that the crofters were losing a battle against the social and economic forces of the day (Adams, 1976: p. 426). Popular critiques of these developments point out that existing legislation tended not only to promote agricultural inefficiency and slow rates of development but that, even if the recommendations were sound economically, they ignored the social and political relationships that had historically developed in the Highlands (Campbell, 1985). The establishment of the Highland and Island Development Board (HIDB) in 1965 was specifically aimed at improving economic and social conditions and facilitating the playing of a more effective role by the Highland people in the development of British industrial capitalism. More recently, a series of oil-related developments have resulted in certain fractions and regions of the Highlands, notably the North-East, experiencing declining and rising rates of employment and an increased allocation of resources.

A number of sociological issues present themselves for resolution as a result of these increased resource implications for the Highlands. Although many of the projects embarked upon by these externally-controlled agencies have been relatively successful over short periods of time, the problems of external control, dependency, cultural domination and fluctuating depopulation rates continued to be key problems of modernity experienced by the Highland social formation. For instance, with regard to oil-related developments, McCrone (1982: p. 47) explores the extent to which dependency upon foreign capital and resources removes the power of decision-making beyond the Highlands. In his discussion on the influence of the HIDB, Grassie (1983: p. 4) indicates that the problems of the relatively autonomous Board are associated with the degree of control exercised at one level by the Scottish Office and at another level by Westminster. The failure of development projects such as the fishing programme, the pulp and paper mill at Fort William, and the aluminium works at Inver Gordon are examples of the fact that, while the projects met the needs of the British state, they were not congruent with the needs and apsirations of the Highland people, many of whom had already been drawn away from the Highlands into a wider urban metropolitan culture.

One other facet of the dependency problems needs to be raised in its

Highland context. As I indicated earlier, the continuing influence of private landlord power is what many social commentators believe to be the key to the continuing social structure of the Highlands (Evans and Hendry, 1985). The precise nature of Highland land-ownership patterns remains uncertain because successive British governments have refused to establish a comprehensive system of land registration. At least two recent studies have indicated that one of the unique features of Highland modernity is the power of a small group of people who, irrespective of their involvement with land as a productive resource, continue to influence local communities. Since 1985 tourists have been invited to spend up to £1 500 per weekend for the privilege of stalking deer with the Duchess of Argyll (*The Sunday Times*, 2 April 1989). Landlords have a continuing influence upon many Highland Gatherings and Games. Yet it is important not to divorce current developments from the past, a past which casts a long shadow in the Highlands in that current land-ownership problems are but a reflection of social transformations which took place during the eighteenth and nineteenth centuries.

Hunter's (1979) relatively recent account asserts that the current Highland landlord class are associated with two centuries of exploitation, depopulation and decay. It is a class, the writer goes on to claim, that deserves to be removed from the land not least because the destruction of Highland landlordism would, more than any other single development, demonstrate that a new and better era had begun in the Highlands (Hunter, 1979: p. 60). In his discussion of the failure of the 'HIDB' to tackle the landlord issue, Grassie (1983: p. 92) asserts that, by 1980, fifteen years after it inception, it had made no progress on the issue that both 'friends and foes alike saw as central to its work'. In deciding to leave the power of the landowner much as it had been for over two hundred years, the Board ultimately ensured, writes Grassie (1983: p. 94), that the status quo would remain. The 'injustices', to use Grassie's (1983: p. 95) words, inflicted by some landowners on the communities dependent upon them, and which had been identified by the HIDB, are allowed to continue.

The study by Housten and Bryden (1976) concluded that some thirty-five families or companies possess no less than one third of the Highland's 7.39 million acres of privately-owned land. Scotland itself consists of 19.5 million acres of which, according to McEwan (1981: p. 9), 16.5 million acres are privately owned by landlords and multinational companies. Some indication of the extent of this dependency is illustrated by McEwan's 1975 figures: 17 individuals or companies own 69 per cent of the land of Caithness; 38 individuals or companies own 84 per cent of the land of Sutherland; 79 individuals or companies own 80 per cent of the land of Ross and Cromarty; and 63 individuals or companies own 62 per cent of the land of Perthshire (McEwan, 1975). Some of the biggest estate owners include the Willis family with 193 700 acres in Ross and Cromarty and Perthshire; the Duke of Atholl, chieftain to the Atholl Highland Games, with 130 000 acres; the Duke of Sutherland, chieftain to various Highland Games, with 123000 acres; the Duke of Baccleuch with 277000 acres and the Duke of Westminster with 120800 acres (McEwan, 1981: p. 11). Highland sporting landlords regularly appear on the list of Britain's richest 2000 people published annually by both *The Sunday Times* and *Money Magazine*.

Multinational companies are also well represented in the 1970s and 1980s. Figures from the Scottish Government Yearbook (1979) indicate that the biggest investors in Highland land included the Enessey Company Limited of Lausanne, Switzerland with its 61000-acre Mar Lodge Estate, its 15 000-acre Tulchan Estate in Moray and its 62 500-acre estate on the Isle of Harris, and the Dubai-based Mohammed Al Fayed whose company, Borcado Societé Anonyme of Lichtenstein, recently bought 3 463 acres in Aberdeenshire (Hunter, 1979). In 1972, James Theodore Cremer, a company director of Nove Zembla Holland, sold land to Cremer Oil Texas for £182 000. In June 1977, the Keir estate in Perthshire was sold to Park Tower Holdings Establishment for £1 900 000, while the Eagle Star Insurance Company bought 18 000 acres in Moray (McEwan, 1981).

The question of the Highland landlords has been raised in this instance as illustrative of the fact that dependency upon a relatively powerful group or social class fraction continues to be one of the key problems of modernity experienced by the Highland social formation. As illustrated earlier it is entirely appropriate to see this discussion on the Highland landlords as relevant to the development of the modern Highland Gatherings. While a degree of democratisation has developed, in a residual sense sporting landlords of the 1990s continue to influence the Highland Gatherings and Games in a number of ways: (i) they still make a significant contribution to the social structure of many modern Highland Gatherings; (ii) they help to produce and reproduce cultural images of a way of life which effectively ended after about 1745. The part played by the Victorian landlords in transforming the social structure of the Highlands is often forgotten in romantic narratives of the past; (iii) the sporting and land management policies of the sporting landlords continue to take relatively little cognisance of the needs of the community; (iv) they contribute to a process of cultural domination by reflecting in part the values of a metropolitan élite; and (v) they contribute to a depopulation process which draws Highlanders into the core centres of the industrial metropolis.

In drawing this chapter together I wish to highlight the core of the analysis and to locate this phase of development within the broader development process. The notion of dominant and residual forms helps to accomplish this task, although it is important to stress that such forms of culture are not independent of the relational arrangements which are the very essence and fabric of these social and sporting forms of practice.

DOMINANT AND RESIDUAL CONCERNS

I have argued throughout this chapter that any discussion on the modern Highland Gatherings and Games must take account of the problems of modernity experienced at different levels by social fractions of the modern Scottish social formation which emerged after about 1920. Although Highland fractions within Scotland may have experienced and resisted problems of dependency in the past, it was not until this period that such problems were experienced by the Scottish social formation as a whole. While it would be inaccurate to assume that the influence of a relatively powerful metropolitan elite did not give rise to a great deal of tension, struggle and flux, no longer were the centripetal forces of the south as ineffective as they had been during the reign of the Canmore kings in the eleventh and twelfth centuries.

Regardless of whether the focus of analysis is at the level of the Highland regional formation or that of the Scottish national formation as a whole, a common problem of modernity is the dependency which has risen out of the power of a metropolitan élite to control the flow of resources both in and out of the Scottish hinterland or periphery. This dynamic dependency relationship has led to the traffic of people, materials and ideas, all of which help to reinforce and resist changing patterns of economic, cultural and political domination and development. Various class, national, Highland and Lowland social fractions have all, at various times, contested an emergent dominant metropolitan hegemony. While various British state policies have attempted to solve many of the problems of modernity, such policies themselves are political and cultural manifestations of the fact that whole communities and ways of life have become dependent upon the decisions taken by various social class fractions who are remote from those people who live out their lives within the Scottish periphery.

Certain pressures and tensions have contributed to a modern expression of the Highland Gatherings and Games. It is an expression which itself is nothing more than a contemporary expression of those groups of people who construct, control and negotiate the values, meanings and practices associated with today's Highland Gatherings and Games. Such a dominant expression has not merely evolved, but has developed out of a number of complex processes and mediation within and between a complete set of dynamic relational arrangements. Nonetheless, for all this complexity, I have tried to illustrate that a dominant interpretation of today's Highland Gatherings and Games is essentially different and yet constituted from many of those earlier traditions and practices of previous interdevelopmental stages. Residual glimpses of earlier social arrangements and practices still partially penetrate the dominant interpretation of the modern Highland Gatherings and Games.

More specifically, increasing commodification, professionalisation, rationalisation, incipient bureaucratisation and relative democratisation are but a few of the many multifaceted developments which have emerged since about 1910. The modern Highland Gatherings and Games continued to experience problems of cultural domination and the production and reproduction of a romantic cultural identity. This in itself contributes to the broader problems of modernity. Expressions of these developments are numerous, with the following being some of the more clear-cut facets of today's Highland Gatherings and Games: advertising, sponsorship and the expansion of a comprehensive consumer culture which exploits many of the kitsch symbols of cultural identity; the relative acceptance of uniform rules, regulations and records under the control of such bureaucracies as the Scottish Games Association; changing class relationships as expressed, for example, at the level of organisational control have led to a degree of democratisation; and the continuing influence and dependency upon a romantic cultural identity, including images of Balmorality. All these facets contribute to a dominant interpretation of the modern Highland Gatherings and Games which itself has been mediated by a number of the broader problems of modernity.

A broad set of residual definitions and interpretations also contribute to the modern Highland Gatherings and Games. The continuing influence of the sporting landlords and vestiges of the Highland clan formation continue to contribute to the modern Highland Gatherings and Games in a residual sense. That is to say, they may have been part of a dominant set of social arrangements which contributed to Highland Gatherings and Games in the past, but are no longer dominant today. These expressions are most prominent at the more traditional Highland Gatherings such as Lonach, Braemar, Aboyne and Glenisla. The Earl of Huntley, the Duke of Argyll, the Duke of Atholl, as respective clan chieftains, and the continuing clan associations, such as the Wallaces, Forbes, Farquharsons, Gunns, McPhersons and Gordons, all continue to reflect a pre-1745 way of life which, although violent at times, materially impoverished, and dependent upon a patriarchal-feudal set of social relations, was essentially egalitarian in that the power of the Highland Chief was subject to a degree of control by the clan. For instance, the land was essentially owned by the clan and not the Highland chief.

Finally, on a more oppositional note, while such residual cultural practices may link the modern Highland Gatherings with a pre-1745 stage of development, the very same residual images also link the modern Highland Gatherings and Games with subsequent developmental stages from about 1740 to about 1850 and from about 1840 to 1920. In the first instance, the Highland way of life was to a large extent destroyed and marginalised and in the second instance, Highland culture was romanticised and incorporated into mainstream British culture. As I have repeatedly indicated throughout this study, the dominant interpretation of the Highland Gatherings and Games includes a romantic cultural identity in which Highland chiefs, clansfolk, landlords and crofters all experienced life in terms of harmonious social relations. There is a very real danger of basking in the crofting clannish image of the past, the implication being that the political, social and economic climate has not change and that the old tactics and demands used in the past would work today. There are many lessons to be learned from the past, but not if the lessons are divorced from the social reality and social context within which they were originally experienced. As a destroyer of myths, the sociologist should strive to achieve a tighter fit between facts and reality. If history and social development were remembered, it would not be a romantic cultural identity which would be perpetuated through such cultural forms as the Highland Gatherings. Indeed, in an oppositional sense, just as Highland culture has been capable of providing the basis of a romantic Scottish cultural identity, it is also capable of providing a basis of counter-hegemonic struggle against the problems of modernity. What is required is not an identity based on a Highland fairytale but one that engages social reality and understands the harsh realities of the clearances, the development of Scotland as a sporting playground and the problems of dependency and underdevelopment experienced within a modern social formation. If history is remembered, then little romantic satisfaction would be gained from such an experience.

5

URBAN POLITICS, SPORTING LANDLORDS AND THE SELECTION OF TRADITION

This study does not claim to provide a comprehensive theoretical discussion or a complete analysis of Highland social development. At a much more basic level this work has been concerned with: (i) providing a theoretically guided analysis of a particular sporting practice; (ii) situating the analysis of sport within the broader context of Scottish and Highland development; and (iii) making a contribution to an ethnocentralistic body of literature on the sociology of sport. Perhaps the relative strength and weakness of this work is that it has attempted to address the interrelated nature of all of these concerns.

More specifically this work has concerned itself with the development of the Scottish Highland Gatherings. I have attempted to illustrate throughout this study that the development of this Highland tradition has paralleled much broader transformations within the Highland and Scottish social formations. The text has encompassed some of the most basic questions that might be asked concerning Scottish cultural identity, dependency and social structure. What is the relationship between the Highland Gatherings and various social groups such as the clan, the landlord and the émigré? What is the relationship between the Highland Gatherings and the prevailing social structure? How have the Highland Gatherings been affected by the historical epoch in which they move? In what ways do the modern Highland Gatherings differ from the traditional Highland Gatherings? Why did the Gatherings suddenly become popular after about 1840? What social forces have shaped this Highland tradition? Who have been the most powerful people within the complex web of interdependent configurations associated with the Highland Gatherings? In what complex ways has this power been expressed in practice? In what ways do these Highland Gatherings reflect Scottish cultural identity?

Such problems have provided a basis for developing an analysis of the Scottish Highland Gatherings which has revolved around four interrelated stages of development. The first stage of development lasted from at least the eleventh century until about 1750. Many of the folk origins of today's modern Highland Gatherings such as hill-racing, playing the piobaireachd, highland dancing and the wearing of tartan dress are all examples of cultural practices which may have been originally located within the development of a patriarchal-feudal set of social relations in which the Highland clan proved to be a particularly important formation. A Highland way of life existed which was essentially relatively violent, materially impoverished and based on a kinship or patriarchal set of social relations modified by feudalism. An essential feature of this Highland way of life was that the Highland clan was dependent upon land being laid out to ensure the continued existence of the clan. The land of the Highland clan was not the private property of the chief but the public property of the clansfolk.

A second stage of development emerged between about 1740 and about 1850. A vast number of factors gave rise to the reorganisation and social upheaval experienced by the Highland people during this period of cultural marginalisation and transformation. These processes were accelerated in the first instance by the post-Culloden policies of the British state which were designed to destroy the social and political fabric of a way of life that had revolved around the Highland clan figuration. The Act of Proscription of 1747 was particularly significant, not merely in that it prevented the wearing of Highland dress, the meeting together of Highland people and the participation in traditional forms of entertainment, but also in that it removed the judicial powers of the Highland chief over his own people. A number of Highland cultural practices, including sporting traditions, developed, particularly in North America, largely in conjunction with the emigration process, a process which resulted from the relatively less powerful, but not powerless, people within the Highland social formation being evicted from the land. Those who remained became increasingly dependent upon the emerging landlord class. By the early part of the nineteenth century, the paradoxical situation had emerged whereby many of the descendants of those Highland landlords and Highland chiefs who had contributed to the demise of the old way of life became responsible for its survival. Divorced from their original social context, the Highland Gatherings experienced problems of cultural marginalisation and subsequent transformation during this period.

From about 1840 until about 1920 a third stage of development evolved. One cannot claim that there was a direct causal link between the financial difficulties in letting and stalking sheep walks but, in association with the glorification of the Highlands as a sporting playground for a specific social élite, it can certainly be argued that the Victorian period led to different forms of resource exploitation that contributed to both the advance of a metropolitan culture and the continuing tension and conflict between the landowners and the Highland tenantry or crofters. The power of the sporting landlord class led not only to the popularisation of the Highland Gatherings and Games, but also to a process of cultural dependency whereby many of the images, practices and traditions that have come to be associated with this particular sporting form continued to be selected, romanticised and attributed different meanings. In particular, two crucial interconnected developments took place between about 1840 and about 1920. In the first place, the Highland Gatherings became inextricably linked with processes of Balmoralisation and popularisation. In this connection Highland dress again became a statutory mode of attire at the Games. Accessories that would have struck the old Highland clansfolk as amazing were incorporated into the outfit. What was particularly significant about the sporting landlord phenomenon was the emergence of various social class fractions, each with a relative degree of economic and social power, alongside the traditional aristocracy. While the Highland Gatherings were experiencing Balmoralisation and popularisation influences, these developments were taking place against a background of tension and struggle between two broad interdependent social fractions, each with a greater or lesser degree of power. Again, questions of dependency and land-ownership lay at the heart of this tension, a tension which, in part, led to the passing of the Crofters Act of 1886.

Since about 1920 to the present day, the modern Highland Gatherings and Games have continued to develop at various rates and in a number of multifaceted ways. Some of the many facets which have contributed to this modern expression are: the fact that the emergence of the professional Highland Gatherings helped to integrate this Highland tradition into the market place and legitimate the phenomenon as an area of open competition and commercial activity; a move towards an incipient bureaucratisation of procedures; the production and reproduction of a romantic cultural identity; various rates of rationalisation; and a general standardisation of rules. Seen in isolation, the differences between the multitude of Highland Gatherings and Games of today may be viewed by many as being insignificant. Yet viewed in the context of long-term development, it is possible to differentiate clearly between the folk origins of this Highland tradition, subsequent phases of development and that which is characteristically modern. In particular, it has been argued in this study that any discussion of the modern Highland Gatherings and Games must be located within the changing nexus and patterns of social arrangements which have resulted from a broad modernisation process in which problems of dependency and cultural domination have given rise to varying rates of flux and tension within the Scottish social formation. What is particularly significant about modern Scotland is the fact that while fractions of the Highland social formation had experienced problems of dependency in the past, such problems were not experienced by the Scottish social formations a whole until after about 1920. The social fabric of the modern Highland Gatherings and Games was influenced by and contributed to this broader modernisation process.

I should like to finish by highlighting a number of crucial points which have been central to the thinking behind this text. Firstly, there is the issue of dependency and uneven development. It has never been the intention to put forward a simplistic economic model as the basis for explaining why Scotland is different. Most Scottish political economists and social historians have generally accepted the relevance of a set of framing assumptions centred on such terms as core or centre, hinterland and periphery and dependence and underdevelopment. Yet the crucial factor is not to exaggerate certain distributional differences and link these to some form of dependency theory, but to articulate the ways in which Scottish political, economic and cultural struggles have arisen out of a particular pattern of historical development. Dependency can only be adequately explained if it turns to the examination of the historically structured relations and conflict between Scotland and the British state and in particular the ways in which a distinct civil society and a distinct cultural identity has developed alongside political control through Westminster. Thus this text has attempted to show, not just that Scotland is different, but that any attempt to explain the origins and nature of this difference must avoid a narrow concentration on just the Scottish economy and instead place its explanation within the context of Scotland's history and its effects on contemporary beliefs and actions.

Secondly, there is the problem of cultural identity and tradition. It has been suggested by Hugh Trevor-Roper (1983) that the Highland tradition is in fact an invented tradition. In particular it is argued that tartanry was hastily contrived towards the end of Queen Victoria's reign. In the context of cultural dependency I would argue that the Highland tradition, and indeed Scottish cultural identity, is not so much an invented tradition as a selection of tradition. Tartans, clans, and a certain way of life did exist prior to about 1745, it was not invented. Various social fractions, such as the Highland landlords, by virtue of their power, selected, interpreted and attributed different meanings to such cultural artefacts as tartanry, clans and what Nairn refers to as the kitsch symbols of Scottish cultural identity. It is important not to divorce such romantic symbols, upon which Scotland has become culturally and to a degree economically dependent, from historically lived experience. At the level of popular culture, not even on Highland Games day, do you see the bulk of the Highland people walking around in kilts, scarfs and other tartan fabrics.

Thirdly, there is the issue of work on Scottish sport and leisure. While Whitson (1983) and Moorehouse (1987) have begun to question and probe the extent to which general theories about the development of sporting traditions and sporting behaviour in Britain might be inadequate when faced with Scottish evidence, within the morass of recent sociological, cultural and historical work on sport the 'peripheral presence' remains noticeable only by its absence. Perhaps the possible value of this work on the Highland Gatherings is that it allows discussions on Scottish sport to be located within much broader debates which have prompted education-alists, sociologists, historians and cultural critics alike to challenge the dominant cultural power, question its values and assumptions and enquire into the complex way in which it mediates Scottish ways of life.

Finally, there is the factor of the sporting landlords. The precise nature of Highland land-ownership patterns remains relatively uncertain because successive British governments have refused to establish a comprehensive system of landownership. One of the many factors which has given rise for concern has been the continuing development and impact of sporting estates in the Highlands. A district interlocking exists, not only between the sporting landlords and the positions of power and influence within the Highland Gatherings, but also between the sporting landlords and Highland social structure in general. Despite the changes brought about by government legislation and the anti-Thatcherite struggle in Scotland, the power of the private landlords remains the keystone to understanding Highland development. Yet while the Scottish political struggles drew heavily upon the memory of Highland rural struggles during the 1920s, Scottish politics in the 1980s and early 1990s have tended to be urban orientated. The Highland land question has been relatively neglected within current Scottish political debates. Yet the power, privilege and wealth of the Highland and sporting landlords remains capable of arousing more passion and fervour than just about any other Scottish political issue. History tells us that Highland problems only rank high on Westminster's agenda when, as happened in the 1880s, Highlanders promoted their own interests. The peripheral status of the Highlands and the power of private landlordism should contribute to a distinctive Scottish socialist force attempting to halt the inroads of Thatcherism and the New Right.

APPENDIX I

OBSERVATION AT A SELECT NUMBER OF HIGHLAND GATHERINGS

Gathering	Date	Venue
Blair Atholl Highland Games	24 May 1895	Blair Atholl
Ceres Highland Games	27 June 1985	Ceres, Fife
Elgin Highland Games	1 July 1985	Elgin, Moray
Dufftown Highland Games	25 July 1985	Dufftown
Taynult Highland Games	26 July 1986	Taynult
Assynt Highland Games	8 August 1986	Lochinver
Ballater Highland Games	14 August 1986	Ballater
Argyllshire Highland Gathering	27 August 1986	Oban
Cowal Highland Gathering	30 August 1986	Dunoon
Blackford Highland Games	31 August 1986	Blackford, Perthshire
Braemar Highland Gathering	6 September 1986	Braemar
Pitlochry Highland Games	13 September 1986	Pitlochry
Atholl Highland Gathering	27 May 1990	Perthshire
Aberdeen Highland Games	17 June 1990	Aberdeen
Grantown-on-Spey Highland Games	24 June 1990	Morayshire

APPENDIX II

Interviews	Date	Location
Trossachs Highland Games, Committee	15 February 1985	Perth
Airth Highland Games, Committee (1)	12 April 1986	Airth
Airth Highland Games, Secretary (2)	12 December 1986	Airth
Cowal Highland Gathering, Secretary	11 June 1986	Dunoon
Braemar Highland Gathering, President	4 July 1986	Braemar
Argyllshire Highland Gathering, Secretary	9 July 1986	Oban
Harlkirk Highland Games, Secretary	6 August 1986	Halkirk
Caol Highland Games, Secretary	6 August 1986	Aberdeen
Ballater Highland Games, President	7 August 1986	Ballater
Glenisla Highland Gathering, Secretary	18 August 1986	Kirriemuir
Lochaber Highland Games, Secretary	18 August 1986	Fort Wiliam
Lonach Highland Gathering, Secretary	20 August 1986	Strathdon
Aberlour & Strathspey Highland Games, Secretary	20 August 1987	Aberlour
Crieff Highland Games, Secretary	17 August 1987	Perth
Grantown-on-Spey Highland Games, Committee	19 August 1987	Moray
Atholl Highland Gathering (various)	27 May 1990	Perthshire
Isle of Seil Highland Games (various)	30 June 1990	Argyll
Caithness Highland Gathering (various)	7 July 1990	Caithness

BIBLIOGRAPHY

1 NEWSPAPERS AND MAGAZINES

Aberdeen Free Press
Annual Book of the Braemar Gatherings
Arbroath Herald Press
Caithness Courier
Dunoon Observer and Argyllshire Standard
Falkirk Herald
Glasgow Herald
Inverness Journal
John O'Groats Journal
Oban Times
The Scotsman
Scottish-American Journal
Scots Magazine
Scottish Field Magazine
West Highland Free Press
Witness

2 REPORTS AND ESTATE PAPERS

Breadalbane Papers, Scottish Record Office, S/R/O
Ellice Papers, National Library of Scotland, N/L/S
Mcleod Papers, Dunvegan, Skye
Old Statistical Accounts of Scotland 1831, N/L/S (S/A/S)
New Statistical Accounts of Scotland 1961, N/L/S
Report of the Commissioners of Inquiry into the Condition of the Crofters and Cottars in the Highlands and Islands of Scotland, Annual Reports 1899-1912, S/R/O
Congested Districts Boards for Scotland, Annual Reports 1899-1912, S/R/O
Report of the Scottish Land Enquiry Commission, 1914, N/L/S
Report of the Departmental Committee appointed to Enquire and Report with regards to Lands in Scotland used as Deer Forests 1922, S/R/O
Report to the Church and Nation Committee, Scottish interests, 1985, N/L/S

3 HIGHLAND GAMES, MINUTES, PROGRAMMES AND UNPUBLISHED PAPERS

3.1 Minutes of the Braemar Royal Highland Society, Braemar
Minutes of the Ballater Athletic Club, Ballater
Minutes of the Glenisla Highland and Friendly Society, Kirriemuir
Minutes of the Halkirk Athletic Club, Halkirk
Minutes of the Newtonmore Highland Games, Banff
Minutes of the Northern Meeting, Inverness

3.2 Programmes from highland gatherings and games:

Aboyne Highland Gathering and Games
Airth Highland Games
Argyllshire Highland Gathering and Games
Assynt Highland Games
Aviemore Highland Games
Ballater Highland Gathering
Braemar Highland Gathering
Cowal Highland Gathering and Games
Dundee Highland Games
Halkirk Highland Games
Invergordon Highland Gathering
Lonach Highland Gathering
Mull Highland Games
Newtonmore Highland Games
Tomintoul Highland Games
Trossachs Highland Games

3.3 Unpublished Papers:

Story of the Airth Highland Games, Airth Highland Games
Committee, Airth
History of the Cowal Highland Gathering, Cowal Highland
Gathering Committee, Dunoon
Halkirk and its Highland Games, Halkirk Highland Games
Committee, Halkirk
History of Tomintoul Highland Games, Dr. J. Warre, Torwood,
Tomintoul

4 BOOKS AND ARTICLES

Abrams, Philip (1982) *Historical Sociology* Somerset, Open Books
Adams Gordon (1976) 'The Highlands Dilemma', *New Society*, 26 February
Anderson, Perry (1980) *Arguments within English Marxism*, London, Verso/
NLB
Anderson, Perry (1979) *Considerations on Western Marxism*, London,
Verso/NLB
Anderson, Perry (1978) *Passages from Antiquity to Feudalism*, London,
Verso/NLB

Alison, Lincoln (1986) *The Politics of Sport* Manchester, Manchester University Press

Armstrong, A. & Mather, A. (1983) *Land Ownership and Land Use in the Scottish Highlands*, Aberdeen, Aberdeen University Press

Barron, J. (1907) *The Northern Highlands in the Nineteenth Century*, Vols. 1-3 Inverness

Birrell, Susan (1978) 'From Ritual to Record, Review', *International Committee for Sociology of Sport Bulletin*, 15 November

Blake, A. (1951) *Barry and the Kailyard School*, London, Barker

Bloomstrom, M. & Hettne, B. (1984) *Development Theory in Transition*, London, Zep Press

Bold, Alan (1983) *Modern Scottish Literature*, New York, Longman

Bottomore, Tom (1984) *Sociology and Socialism*, Brighton, Harvester Press

Brander, Michael (1982) *The Emigrant Scots*, London, Constable

Brown, Gordon (1975) *Red Paper on Scotland*, Edinburgh, EUSPB

Brown, P. H. (1843) *Scotland before 1700 from Contemporary Documents*, Edinburgh

Browne, J. (1849) *A History of the Highlands and of the Highland Clans*, Vols. 1-4, Edinburgh

Bumsted, J. M. (1982) *The People's Clearances, 1770-1815*, Edinburgh, Edinburgh University Press

Burgess, Keith (1980) 'Scotland and the First British Empire, 1707-1770s: the Confirmation of client Status' in Tony Dickson (ed.), *Scottish Capitalism, Class, State and Nation from before the Union to the Present*, London, Lawrence and Wishart

Burnett, Ray (1985) 'Highland Land Raids: Their Contemporary Significance' in Irene Evans and Joy Hendry (eds.), *The Land for the People*, Perthshire, Scottish Socialist Society

Burnett, Ray (1984) 'Land Raids and the Scottish Left', *Centrastus* No. 18, Autumn

Burt, Edward (1815) *Letters from a Gentleman in the North of Scotland*, London

Callender, R. F. (1987) *A Pattern of Landownership in Scotland*, Finzean, Haughend

Campbell, Duncan (1985) 'The Real Crisis of Scottish Agriculture' in D. McCrone (ed.), *Scottish Government Yearbook*, Edinburgh, Harrison, Rowan and Littlefield

Cannadine, David (1983) 'The Context, Performance and Meaning of Ritual: The British Monarchy and the Invention of Tradition' in Eric Hobsbawn and Terence Ranger (eds.), *The Invention of Tradition*, Cambridge, Cambridge University Press

Cardoso, F. E. (1972) 'Dependency and Under-development in Latin America' in *New Left Review* No. 74, July

Cardoso, F. & Faletto, E. (1969) *Dependencia Y Desarollo en America Latina*, Mexico, Siglo

Carnell, Francis Drake (1939) *It's an Old Scottish Custom*, London, Peter Davies

Carter, Ian (1976) 'Kailyard: The Literature of Decline in Nineteenth Century Scotland' in *Scottish Journal of Sociology* Vol. 1, No. 1, November pp. 1-13

Carter, Ian (1974) 'The Highlands of Scotland as an Underdeveloped Region' in Kadt and Williams (eds.), *Sociology and Development*, London, Tavistock

Chapman, Malcolm (1979) *The Gaelic Vision in Scottish Culture*, London, Croom Helm

Chilicote, H. (1974) 'Dependency: A Critical Synthesis of the Literature' in *Latin American Perspectives* Vol. 1

Clarke, J. & Critcher, C. (1985) *The Devil Makes Work: Leisure in Capitalist Britain*, London, Macmillan

Colquhoun, I. & Machell, H. (1927) *Highland Gatherings*, London, Heath Cranton Ltd

Cowan, Edward (1980) *The People's Past*, Edinburgh, Polygon Books

Creegan, E. (1969) 'The Tacksmen and their Success' in *Scottish Studies* Vol. XIII

Critcher, C. & Clarke, J. (1981) 'Sociology of Leisure: Review of the Conventional Wisdom' in Alan Tomlinson (ed.), *Leisure and Social Control*, Brighton

Cunningham, A. (1932) *The Loyal Clans*, Cambridge, Cambridge University Press

Dickson, T. & Clarke, T. (1982) 'The Making of a Class Society: Commercialisation and Working-Class Resistance 1780-1830' in Tony Dickson (eds.), *Scottish Capitalism, Class, State and nation from before the Union to the Present*, London, lawrence and Wishart

Dickinson, W. C., Donaldson, G. D. & Milne, I. A. (1952) *A Source Book of Scottish History*, Vols. 1-3, Edinburgh, Thomas Nelson

Donaldson, Emily-Ann (1986) *The Scottish Highland Games in America*, Gretna, Pelican

Donaldson, M. (1926) *Further Wanderings Mainly in Argyll*, Paisley, Alexander Gardner

Duff, Hart-Davis (1978) *Monarchs of the Glen*, London, Macmillan

Dummet, Alan (1973) *Portrait of English Racism*, Harmondsworth, Penguin

Dunning, Eric (1989) 'Sport in the Civilizing Process: Aspects of the Figurational Approach to Sport and Leisure' in Chris Rojek (ed.), *Leisure for Leisure: Critical Essays*, London, Macmillan

Dunning, Eric (1981) 'The Sociology of Sport in Europe and the United States: Critical Observations from an Eliasian Perspective' in North American Society for Sport Sociology *Conference Proceedings*, Fort Worth, Texas

Dunning, Eric (1971) *The Sociology of Sport*, London, Frank Cass

Dunning, E. & Sheard, K. (1979) *Barbarians, Gentlemen and Players*, Oxford, Martin Robertson & Co.

Durkheim, Emile (1933) *The Division of Labor*, New York, Macmillan

Durkheim, Emile (1915) *The Elementary Forms of Religious Life* (trans J. Swain), London

Elias, Norbert (1987) *Involvement and Detachment*, Oxford, Basil Blackwell

Elias, Norbert (1983) *The Court Society*, Oxford, Basil Blackwell

Elias, Norbert (1982) *State Formation and Civilization*, Oxford, Basil Blackwell

Elias, Norbert (1978a) *What is Sociology?* Basil Blackwell

Elias, Norbert (1978b) *The Civilizing Process*, Oxford, Basil Blackwell

Elias, Norbert (1956) 'Problems of Involvement and Detachment' in *British Journal of Sociology*, No. 7

Elias, N. & Dunning, E. (1986) *Quest for Excitement*, Oxford, Basil Blackwell

Evans, I. & Hendry, J. (1985) *The Land for the People*, Perthshire, Scottish Socilaist Society

Fairhurst, Horace (1967) 'The Rural Settlement Pattern of Scotland, with special reference to the West and North' in Steel, R. and Lawton, R. (eds.), *Liverpool Essays in Geography*, London

Ferguson, Adam (1767) *Essay on the History of Civil Society*, Edinburgh

Ferguson, John (1984) 'Scotland's Periphery' *Cencrastus*, No. 16, Spring

Foster-Carter, Aidan (1985) 'The Sociology of Development' in Michael Haralambos (ed.), *Sociology: New Directions*, Ormskirk, Causeway Press Ltd

Foucault, Michael (1975) *Discipline and Punish*, Harmondsworth, Penguin

Frank, A. G. (1984) *Critique and Anti-Critique: Essays on Dependence and Reformism*, London, Macmillan Press

Frank, A. G. (1967) *Capitalism and Under-development in Latin America*, New York, Monthly Review Press

Gallagher, Tom (1989) 'National Identity and the Working Class in Scotland' in *Cencrastus*, No. 33, Spring

Giddens, Anthony (1971) *Capitalism and Modern Social Theory*, Cambridge, Cambridge University Press

Grant, Elizabeth (1898) *Memoirs of a Highland Lady*, London, Murray

Grant, Isobel (1961) *Highland Folk Ways*, London, Routledge and Kegan Paul

Grant, Isobel (1930) *The Social and Economic Development of Scotland before 1603*, Edinburgh, Oliver and Boyd.

Grassie, James (1983) *Highland Experiment*, Edinburgh, Polygon Books

Gray, Malcolm (1957) *The Highland Economy, 1750-1850*, Edinburgh, Oliver and Boyd

Gregory, Donald (1836) *History of the Western Highlands of Scotland*, London

Grigor, I. F. (1979) *Mightier than a Lord: The Highland Crofter's Struggle for the Land*, Stornoway, Acair Limited

Gruneau, Richard (1983) *Class, Sport and Social Development*, Amherst, University of Massachussetts Press

Gruneau, Richard (1979) 'Power and Play in Canadian Social Development', *Working Papers in the Sociological Study of Sport and Leisure*, Vol. 2, No. 1, Queens University

Gruneau, R. & Albinson, J. (1976) *Canadian Sport: Sociological Perspectives*, Toronto, Addison-Wesley

Guttmann, Alan (1978) *From Ritual to Record*, New York, Columbia University Press

Hargreaves, Jennifer (ed.), (1982) *Sport, Culture and Ideology*, London, Routledge and Kegan Paul

Hargreaves, John (1986) *Sport, Power and Culture*, Cambridge, Polity Press

Hargreaves, John (1982a) 'Sport, Culture and Ideology' in Jennifer Hargreaves (ed.), *Sport, Culture and Ideology*, London, Routledge and Kegan Paul

Hargreaves, John (1982b) 'Sport and Hegemony: Some Theoretical Problems' in H. Cantelon and R. Gruneau (eds.), *Sport, Culture and the Modern State*, Toronto, University of Toronto Press

Hawker, Peter (1893) *The Diary of Colonel Peter Hawker*, Bath, Kingsmead

Hobsbawn, E. & Ranger, T. (1983) *The Invention of Tradition*, Cambridge, Cambridge University Press

Hobsbawn, Eric (1983) 'Introduction: Inventing Traditions' in E. Hobsbawn & T. Ranger (eds.), *The Invention of Tradition*, Cambridge, Cambridge University Press

Hollands, Robert (1984) 'The Role of Cultural Studies and Social Criticism in the Sociological Study of Sport' in *Quest*, No. 36, 1984

Holt, Richard (1989) *Sport and the British: A Modern History*, Oxford University Press

Horne, J., Jary, D. & Tomlinson, A. (1987) *Sport, Leisure and Social Relations* London, Routledge and Kegan Paul

Houston, G. & Bryden, I. (1976) *Agrarian Change in the Scottish Highlands*, Oxford, Martin Robertson & Co

Hunter, James (1981) 'The Year of the Emigre' in the *Bulletin of Scottish Politics*, No. 2, Spring

Hunter, James (1979) 'The Crofter, the Laird and the Agrarian Socialist: The Highland Land Question in the 1970s in N. Drucker & H. M. Drucker (eds.), *Scottish Government Year Book* 1979, Edinburgh, Harrison and Littlefield

Hunter, James (1976) *The Making of the Crofting Community*, Edinburgh, John Donald

Ingham, Alan (1975) 'Occupational Subcultures in the Work World of Sport' in D. Ball and J. W. Loy (eds.), *Sport and Social Order*, Reading, Addison-Wesley

Innes, J. (1978) 'Shinty: facing up to the New Challenges' in *North* 7, 25

Jarvie, Grant (1989) 'Sport, Highland Gatherings and Cultural Form' in *Cencrastus*, No. 32, Autumn

Jarvie, Grant (1986a) 'Highland Gatherings, Sport and Social Class' in *Sociology of Sport*, Vol. 3, No. 4, December

Jarvie, Grant (1986b) 'Dependency, Cultural Identity and Sporting Landlords' in *British Journal of Sports History*, Vol. 3, No. 1, May

Jarvie, Grant (1985) *Class, Race and Sport in South Africa's Political Economy*, London, Routledge Kegan and Paul

Johnson, Samuel (1924) *Journey to the Western Islands of Scotland*, Oxford

Kando, Thomas (1975) *Leisure and Popular Culture in Transition*, St Louis, Molby & Co.

Kellas, James (1986) *Modern Scotland*, London, Pall Mall

Keltie, John (1885) *The Scottish Highlands*, Vols. 1-2, Edinburgh, Grange

Laclau, Ernesto (1971) 'Feudalism and Capitalism in Latin America' in *New Left Review*, No. 67

Lenin, V. (1967) *Collected Works*, Vol. 1, Moscow, Moscow Publishers

Lennman, Bruce (1977) *An Economic History of Modern Scotland*, London, Batsford

Leys, Colin (1983) *Politics in Britain*, London, Heinemann Educational Books

Leys, Colin (1977a) 'Notes on Dependency Theory', Unpublished papers, Queens University Library, Kingston, Ontario, Canada

Leys, Colin (1977b) 'Underdevelopment and Dependency Theory: Critical Notes' in *Journal of Contemporary Asia*, Vol. 7, No. 1

Logan, James (1876) *The Scottish Gael*, Vol. 1, Inverness, Hugh Mackenzie

Love, J. (1980) 'Raul Prebisch and the Origins of the Doctrine of Unequal Exchange' in *Latin America Research Review*, Vol. 15, No. 1

Lukàcs, G. (1975) *The Historical Novel*, London, Merlin Press

Lukes, Steven (1977) *Essays in Social Theory*, London, Macmillan Press

MacAoidh, Aonghas (1833) *Highland Bagpipe Music*, Aberdeen

Maclaren, Ian (1896) *Kate Carnegie and Those Ministers*, London, Hodder and Stoughton

Maclaren, C. J. (1959) *The Highlands*, London, Batsford

Macleod, R. C. (1927) *The Island Clans During Six Centuries*, Inversness, Carruthers

Marini, R. M. (1972) 'Brazilian sub-imperialism' in *Monthly Review*, February

Martin, M. (1884) *A Description of the Western Isles of Scotland*, Glasgow, Thomas

Marx, Karl (1976) *Preface and Introduction to a Critique of Political Economy*, Peking, Foreign Language Press

Marx, Karl (1962) *Selected Works*, Vol. 2, Moscow, Moscow Publishers

Mark, K. & Engels, F. (1980) *Selected Works*, New York, International Publishers

Mason, Tony (1988) *Sport in Britain*, London, Faber and Faber

McConnochie, Alexander (1895) *Deeside*, Aberdeen, Bissett & Co

McConnochie, Alexander (1923) *The Deer and Deer Forests of Scotland*, London, Witherby

McEwan, John (1981) *Who Owns Scotland?* Edinburgh, EUSPB

McEwan, John (1975) 'Highland Landlordism' in G. Brown (ed.), *Red papers on Scotland*, Edinburgh, EUSPB

Mcpherson, Margaret (1985) 'Crofters and the Crofters Commission' in

Irene Evans and Joy Hendry (eds.), *The Land for the People*, Perthshire, Darien Books

McCrone, David (1982) 'The Social Structure of Modern Scotland' in David McCrone (ed.), *Scottish Government Year Book 1982*, Edinburgh, Harrison and Littlefield

McCrone, D. Kendrick, S. & Straw, P. (1989) *The Making of Scotland: Nation, Culture and Social Change*, Edinburgh, Edinburgh University Press

Merquior, J. G. (1985) *Foucault*, London, Fontan

Mears, Robert (1986) 'A Sociological Analysis of Welsh Nationalism', unpublished Ph.D., University of Leicester

Mills, C. Wright (1981) *The Sociological Imagination*, Cambridge, Cambridge University Press

Mitchell, James (1883) *Reminiscences of Life in the Highlands*, London

Mitchinson, Rosalind (1982) *A History of Scotland*, London, Methuen

Moorehouse, H. F. (1987) 'Scotland Against England: Football and Popular culture' in *International Journal of the History of Sport*, No. 4

Moorehouse, H. G. (1984) 'Professional Football and Working Class Culture: English Theories and Scottish Evidence' in *The Sociological Review*, Vol. 32, No. 2, May

Murray, W. (1984) *The Old Firm Sectarianism, Sport and Society*, Edinburgh, John Donald

Nairn, Tom (1988) *The Enchanted Glass: Britain and its Monarchy*, London, Radius

Nairn, Tom (1981) *The Break up of Britain*, London, Verso/NLB

Orr, Willie (1982) *Deer Forests, Landlords and Crofters*, Edinburgh, John Donald

Orwell, George (1970) *Collected Essays, Journalism and Letters*, Vol. VI, Hammondsworth, Penguin

Panitch, Leo (1981) 'Dependency Theory' in *Canadian Journal of Political Economy*, No. 13

Pennant, T. (1774) *A Tour of Scotland and a Voyage to the Hebrides*, Warrington

Perlman, F. (1970) *The Incoherence of the Intellectual*, Detroit, Black and Red

Pia, Simon (1987) 'Scottish Football' in *Cencrastus*, No. 27, Autumn

Poulantzas, Nicos (1978) *State, Power, Socialism*, London, NL Books

Poulantzas, Nicos (1975) *Political Power and Social Classes*, London, NL Books

Prebble, John (1985) *Culloden* Middlesex, Penguin Books

Prebble, John (1984) *The Highland Clearances*, Middlesex, Penguin Books

Prebisch, R. (1950) *The Economic Development of Latin America and its Principle Problems*, New York, United Nations

Randall, W. & Theobald, R. (1985) *Political Change and Underdevelopment*, London, Macmillan

Redmond, G. (1982) *The Sporting Scots of Nineteenth Century Canada*, Toronto, Associated University Press

Richards, G. (1982) *A History of the Highland Clearances, Agrarian Transformation and the Eviction, 1746-1886*, Vols. 1-2, London, Croom Helm

Rojek, C. (1989) *Leisure for Leisure: Critical Essays*, London, Macmillan

Rojek, C. (1986) 'Problems of involvement and detachment in the writings of Norbert Elias' in *British Journal of Sociology*, Vol. XXVII, No. 4, December

Rojek, C. (1985) *Capitalism and Leisure Theory*, London, Tavistock

Roxburgh, Ian (1979) *Theories of Underdevelopment*, London, Macmillan

Scott, Walter (1814) *Waverley*, Edinburgh, Nelson & Sons

Skene, W. F. (1837) *Chronicles of the Picts and Scots*, Edinburgh

Skocpol, Theda (1984) *Vision and Method in Historical Sociology*, Cambridge, Cambridge University Press

Smout, T. C. (1986) *A Century of the Scottish People 1830-1950*, London, Collins

Smout, T. C. (1981) *A History of the Scottish People 1560-1830*, London, Fontana

Somers, R. (1887) *Letters from the Highlands – 1846*, Inverness

Stewart, David (1822) *Sketches of the Highlanders of Scotland*, Vol. 1, Edinburgh

Sugden, John (1989) 'Fostering Division Through the Three Football Codes', University of Belfast International Sports Symposia

Sugden, J. & Bairner, A. (1986) 'Northern Ireland: Sport in a Divided Society' in Alison, L. (ed.), *The Politics of Sport*, Manchester, Manchester University Press

Sunkel, O. (1969) 'National Development Policy and External Dependency in Latin America' in *Journal of Development Studies*, Vol. 1, No. 1

Sunkel, O. & Paz, P. (1972) 'Big Business and Dependencia' in *Foreign Affairs*, April

Tomlinson, Alan (ed.) (1981) *Leisure and Social Control*, Brighton, Chelsea School

Tonnies, Ferdinand (1963) *Community and Association*, London, Routledge and Kegan Paul

Trevor-Roper, H. (1983) 'The Invention of Tradition: The Highland Tradition of Scotland' in Eric Hobsbawn and Terence Ranger (eds.), *The Invention of Tradition*, Cambridge, Cambridge University Press

Victoria (1868) *Scottish Diaries of Queen Victoria 1840 to 1861*, Midlothian, N/L/S

Wallerstein, I. (1980) *The Modern World System*, Vol. II, London, Academic Press

Wallerstein, I. (1974) *The Modern World System*, Vol. I, London, Academic Press

Webster, David (1973) *The Scottish Highland Games*, Edinburgh, Reprographia

Webster, David (1959) *The Scottish Highland Games*, Glasgow, Collins

Whitson, David (1983) 'Pressure on Regional Games in a Dominant Metropolitan Culture; the Case of Shinty' in *Leisure Studies*, Vol. 2, No. 2, May

Williams, Raymond (1981) *Keywords*, London, Fontana

Williams, Raymond (1977) *Marxism and Literature*, Oxford, Oxford University Press

Yorke, Percy (1821) *Three Nights in Perthshire*, Glasgow

Young, James (1979) *The Rousing of the Scottish Working Class*, London, Croom Helm

Youngson, A. J. (1973) *After the Forty Five*, Edinburgh, Edinburgh University Press

INDEX

Aboyne Highland Gathering, 2, 35, 73
agrarian economy, 28–32
Airth Highland Games, 83–4
anglicisation, 16–22
anglo-saxons, 17, 19
anglo-Scottish relations, ii
Argyll, Duke of, 35, 85
Argyllshire Highland Gathering, 75–7, 84–5
aristocracy, 65–8
Atholl, Duke of, 35

Ballater, Highland Games, 74–5
Balmoral, 63, 66, 67, 76, 99, 103
balance of power, 28
Barron, J., 64
Baxter, Jim, ii
Blake, G., 72
Bold, Alan, 71
Braemar, i, 2, 5, 6, 11, 20–2, 86–7
Browne, J., 7, 18
Bumsted, J., 47, 49, 50, 54
bureaucracy, 87
Burnett, Ray, 78, 80
Burgess, Keith, 44
Burt, Edward, 32, 39

Caermarthen, Marquis of, 6
Carter, Ian, 72
cattle raiding, 22, 27, 30
Ceann-Mor, Malcolm, 6, 7, 17, 18, 21
centrifugal forces, 19, 23, 90
chieftains, Highland, 11, 29
clans, social structure, 11, 27, 28, 32–40, 102
Clarke, J., 1
classical tradition, 1
clearances, Highland, 68–71, 102
Clydeside, 80, 93–5
Colquhoun, I., and Machell, I., 3, 5, 6, 7, 8, 20, 68, 69

commercialisation, 2, 83, 87
Comrie Highland Games, 10
Cosgrove, Stuart, 1
Cowal Highland Gathering, 2, 35, 82–3
Craig Chonnich, 6, 7, 8, 20–2
creach, 27–9, 31
Creegan, E., 53
Crieff Highland Games, 10
Critcher, C., 1
crofters' struggle, 11, 39, 40, 62, 69, 77–80
Crofters Act, 63, 78, 79, 80, 103
Culloden, 9, 18, 32, 34, 40
Cumming, Sir William, 5
culture, 24, 35, 68, 72, 93, 102
critique of high and low culture, 24
cultural identity, iii, 24–6, 37, 71, 72, 80, 90–3, 98–105
cultural marginalisation, ii, 43–6
cultural transformation, ii, 43–61

dependency, 1, 10, 12–14, 63, 81–100, 103, 105
Dickson, Tony, 48, 50, 89, 90, 94
dominant and residual, 98–100
Dunning, Eric, iii, 1, 87
Durkheim, Émile, 68
druids, 9

Elias, Norbert, 5, 10, 11, 19, 23, 50, 86, 92, 93
émigré, 2, 11, 47–56, 91, 101
ethnocentralism, 1, 101
Evans, Joy, 96

famine, 63
feudal control, 18, 19, 32–42
figuration, 14, 18, 22, 33, 68
flockmasters, 70, 78
folk origins of Highland Gatherings, ii, 16–41, 101, 102

Fordun, Ian, 22
foreign investment, 95
Foster, Carter, 14

gaelic language, 24, 45
gathering of the clans, 28, 29, 30
glamour of backwardness, 63–70
Glenelg Highland Gathering, 2
Glenisla Highland Gathering, 2, 72, 73
Goldie, G., 11
Grant, Isobel, 7, 56, 59
Gray, M., 46
Gruneau, Richard, 1, 52, 82

Halkirk Highland Games, 77, 85–6
Hall, Stuart, 14
Hargreaves, John, 1, 82
Harvey, Jean, 1, 82
Hawker, P., 63
hegemony, 17, 24, 40, 68, 98
hereditary power, 34–5
highland clan formation, 22, 32–42
hill-running, 6, 20, 21
historiography, 2, 15–100
Hobsbawn, Eric, 14
Holt, Richard, 1, 2, 82
Horne, John, 1
Humes, 22
Hunter, John, 32, 49, 50, 56, 63, 69, 78, 89, 96,97

invention of tradition, 3, 9, 25–27, 104
Irish Land Act, 79
Irish Scots, 17

Johnson, Samuel, 15

kailyard, 70, 71, 72, 91–2
Kellas, J., 89
Keltie, J., 24, 25
Kinlock, Sir David, 5
kinship, 10

labour relations, 3, 19, 93, 94
landlords, 7, 10, 11, 26, 29, 62–79, 97, 101, 102, 105
landownership, 33, 34, 39, 62, 64, 96–7, 104, 105
Lenman, B., 94
Lonach Highland Gathering, 35
lowland formation, 19, 22–32
Lord of the Isles, 38–40
luchdtack, 35
Luss Highland Gathering, 3

MacAoidh, A., 34, 36
McConnachie, A., 65, 66, 71, 73, 74, 75
McCrone, D., iii, 95
MacCrummens, 36–7
Macdonalds, 11, 22, 38, 41
McEwan, J., 85, 96, 97
MacIntyres, 36
Mackays, 11, 22, 36, 41
MacKenzies, 11, 36, 41
Mackintoshes, 22
Malmesbury, Earl of, 64
Martin, M., 32
Marxists, 43, 70
Miliband, Ralph, i
Mitchell, John, 66
Modern Highland Gatherings, iii, 2, 81–100
Modern Scotland, 89–100
monarchy, 11, 17, 34, 56, 68, 70
Moorehouse, R., 104
mythology, destruction of, 15

Nairn, Tom, 14, 68, 90, 91, 92
Napier Commission, 78–9
nationalism, 60, 89, 90–2
Norsefolk, 17
Northern Meeting, 4–5, 10

oil developments, 89, 90, 97
Orr, W., 77, 78

patriarchy, 20, 24, 32–42, 65
patronage, 6
Pia, Simon, 81
picts, 9, 16, 17
piobaire, 36–9
popular culture, 21
popularisation of the Highlands, 71–8
potato famine, 63
Poulantzas, N., 14
poverty, 63, 89
power, ii, 11–14, 46, 79, 80, 95, 96, 97, 105
    to define history, 15
    and dependency, 11–14
    feudal, 32–42
    patriarchal, 32–42
    and social class, 14
Prebble, J., 45, 47, 50, 58, 69
professionalism, ii, 98

Rebellion, 1745, 5, 9, 23
Redmond, G., iii, 55
Richards, Eric, 30, 39, 48, 58
Roman and Greek culture, 3

romanticism, 7, 61, 72, 100, 104

Scott, Walter, 59, 60
Scottish culture and sport, i–iii, 1–2, 81
Smout, T., 34, 39, 40, 94
social class, iii
    and the landlords, 5, 10, 63
    and power, 10, 88, 89
social development, i, ii, 101, 104
social differentiation, 18, 32–40
social structure of the clan, 32–8
social welfare, 5, 6, 7
sociology of sport, 1–2, 101
sporting estates, 103, 105
staples, 30–1, 63
Stewart, D., 34, 40, 45
superstition, 24–5
symbolism, 67

tacksmen, 11, 32, 39, 53

tartanry, 2, 15, 25–6, 64, 68, 71, 91–2,
    104
theory and evidence, ii, 2–12
tradition, 12, 13, 14, 15, 21, 25–7, 104
Trevor-Roper, H., 25, 68, 104
Trossachs Highland Gathering, 31

unification, 16–22

voluntarism, i, 49, 52
Victoria, Queen, 6, 64–8, 71, 80, 104

Webster, D., 8, 9, 10–12, 20, 75
Whitson, D., 1, 88, 104
wild Scots, 22–32

Yorke, P., 31
Young, S., 93
Youngson, A., 44